W9-AQC-834
ST. MARY'S CITY, MARYLAND 20686

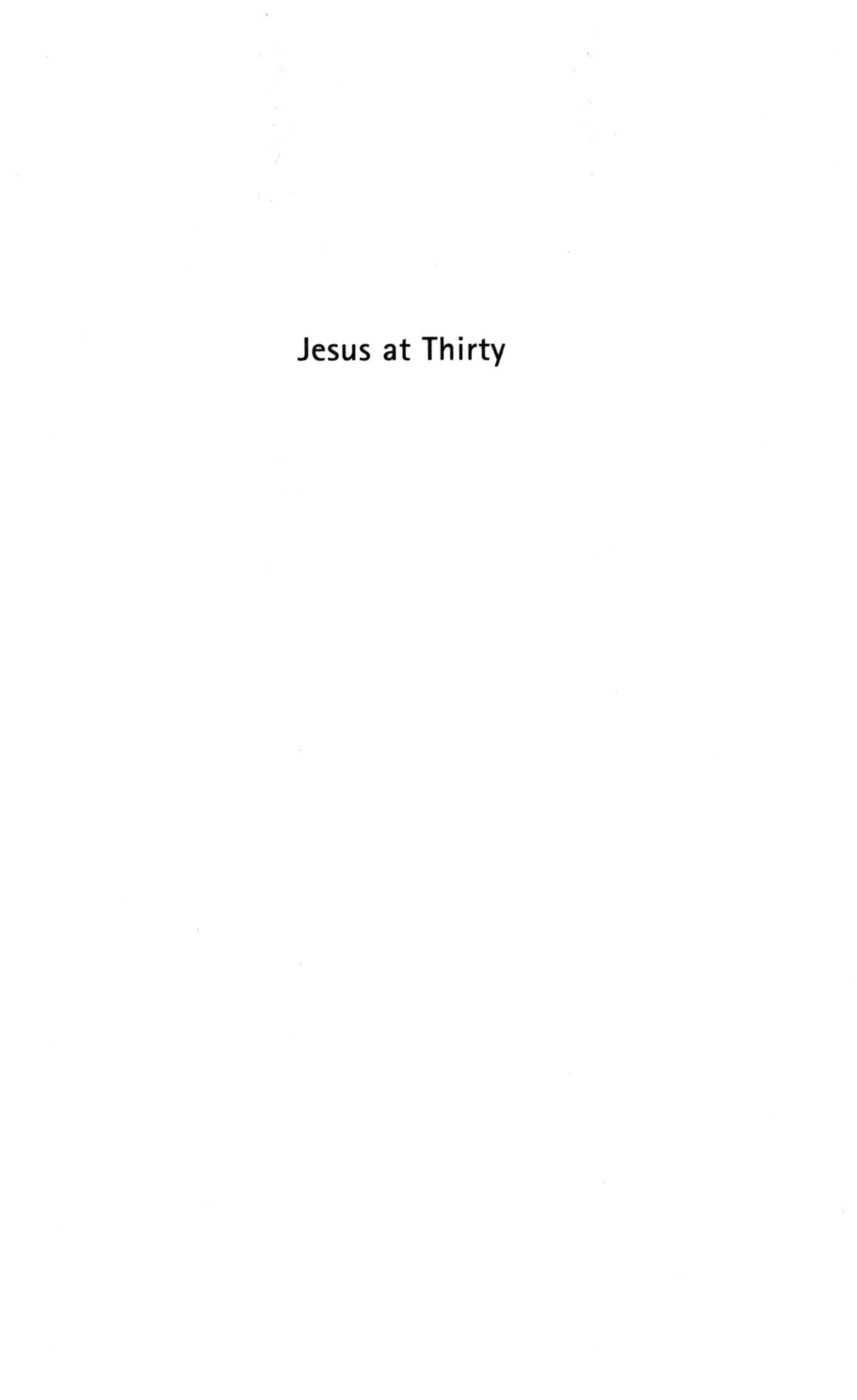

Jesus at Thirty

Jesus at Thirty

A Psychological and Historical Portrait

John W. Miller

Fortress Press
Minneapolis

JESUS AT THIRTY
A Psychological and Historical Portrait

Copyright © 1997 Augsburg Fortress. All rights reserved. Except for brief quotations in critical articles or reviews, no part of this book may be reproduced in any manner without prior written permission from the publisher. Write to: Permissions, Augsburg Fortress, Box 1209, Minneapolis MN 55440.

Scripture quotations unless otherwise noted are from the Revised Standard Version of the Bible, copyright © 1946, 1952, 1971 by the Division of Christian Education of the National Council of Churches. Used by permission.

Book and jacket design by Joseph Bonyata.

Cover art: *Head of Christ* by Annibale Carracci. Used by permission of Staatliche Kunstsammlungen, Dresden, Germany.

Library of Congress Cataloging-in-Publication Data

Miller, John W., 1926–
Jesus at thirty : a psychological and historical portrait / John W. Miller
p. cm.
Includes bibliographical references
ISBN 0-8006-3107-2 (alk. paper)
1. Jesus Christ–Psychology I. Title
BT590.P9M55 1997
232.9'01—dc21 97–23723
CIP

The paper used in this publication meets the minimum requirements of American National Standards for Information Sciences—Permanence of Paper for Printed Library Materials, ANSI Z329.48.1984.

Manufactured in the U.S.A. AF 1-3107

02 01 00 99 98 97 1 2 3 4 5 6 7 8 9 10

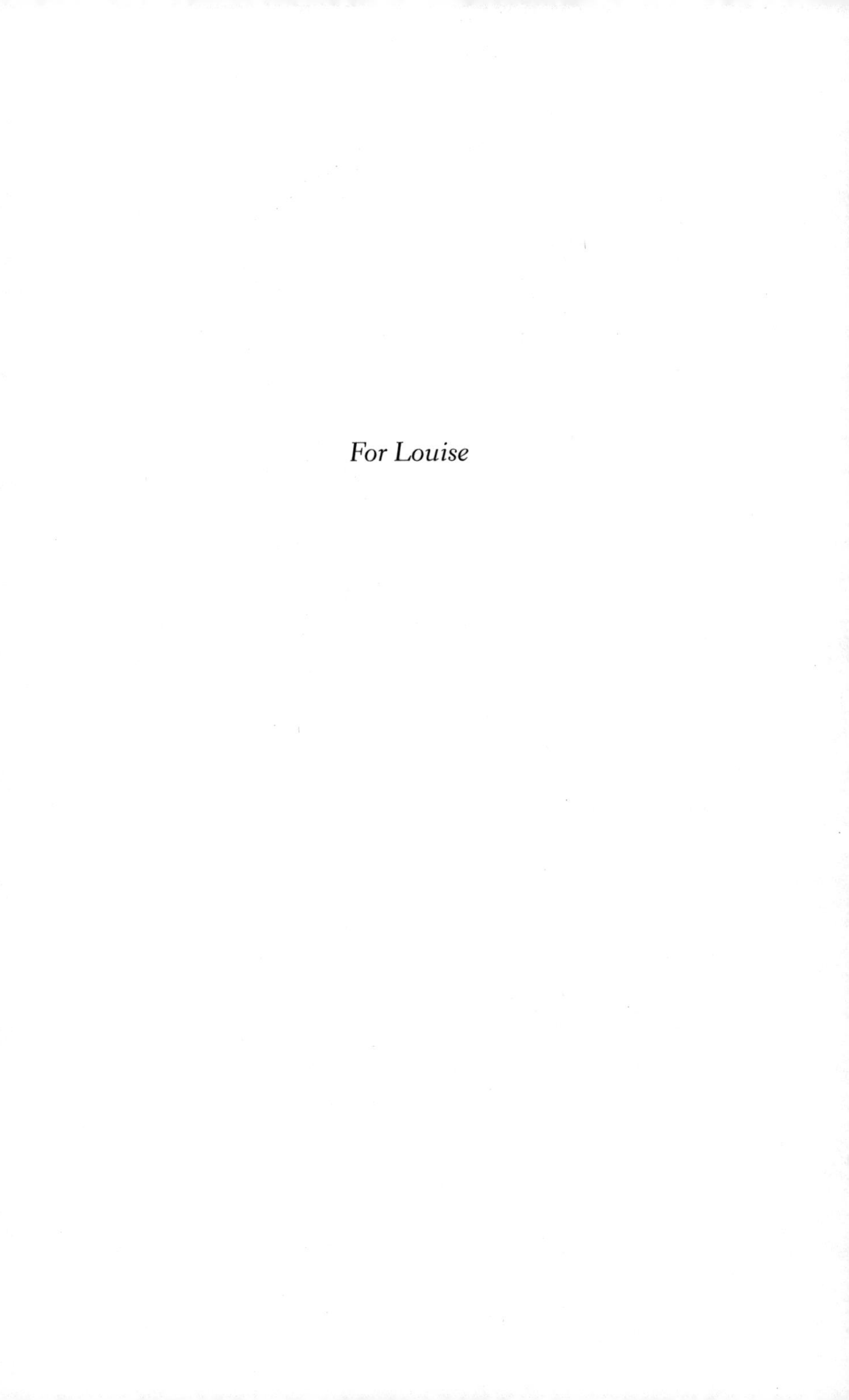

For Louise

Contents

Although he was a Son,
he learned obedience
through what he suffered.

Hebrews 5:8

Preface

Through the centuries the portraits of Jesus have varied from age to age and place to place: "good shepherd" during the early church persecutions; "cosmic ruler" during the triumph of Christianity in the Roman Empire; "the crucified" in the guilt-ridden late Middle Ages.[1] In an age acutely conscious of psychological issues, and now increasingly focused on the developmental challenges and needs of men in particular, my hope is that a psychohistorical inquiry of the kind undertaken here may put us in touch with yet another facet of Jesus' historic achievement—that of "the tempted one" who at the right moment found a wise mentor, humbled himself in baptism, said no to grandiosity, and went on to become what he was meant to be: the prototypically caring, faith-inspiring "generative man" (to borrow a term from Erik Erikson). Such a focus is not absolutely new, since the New Testament Letter to the Hebrews speaks similarly of a Jesus who was tempted (Heb. 4:15) yet triumphed and matured through the things that he suffered (Heb. 5:8).

Until recently, however, knowledge of the earlier stages of human development was limited; this gave rise to biographies that were typically long at the end (in their accounts of an adult's achievements) and short at the beginning (in their accounts of the traumas and triumphs of childhood and youth that may lie behind those accomplishments). The New Testament Gospels illustrate this tendency with their almost total concentration on Jesus' climactic mission in the final year or so of his life. And yet, even here, information regarding developmental antecedents is not altogether lacking, for they do inform us that he was born into a certain kind of family at a certain time and place and for many years worked at a certain occupation, and that it was not until he was "about thirty" that he left home for the Jordan, where he was baptized by a certain type of man and then experienced certain "temptations"—and that not even then did he launch his own unique mission, but only after the one who had baptized him was arrested.

In an age preoccupied with history and steeped in the awareness of how individuals develop psychologically, even this bare outline of a "life" cries out for psychohistorical assessment and reflection. But is it not presumptuous to try to plumb the depths of the inner world of a historically distant figure like Jesus about whom so very little is known, when psychologists or psychoanalysts are often hard pressed to understand the client right in front of them? This dismissive, frequently posed question seriously misconstrues the aims and ambitions of the psychohistorian.[2] Developmental psychology (which seeks to inform us regarding the genesis of aspects of our emotionality) simply offers the historian another way of looking at whatever facts are available for whatever insights can be garnered from viewing them in this light. Thus, even the most fragmentary data (name, place and date of birth, names of parents and siblings, vocation, time of marriage) may be approached from a psychohistorical angle for the very same reason that a historian might examine it with the help of insights from linguistics, archaeology, economics, religion, or sociology.[3] Of course, when a field of research as complex as developmental psychology is resorted to for understanding texts as multifaceted and ambiguous as those we must contend with in modern Jesus research, we cannot hope for conclusions as firm or specific as might result from the study of someone for whom the primary sources are historically more straightforward or emotionally illuminating.

My motives for undertaking this project and the psychohistorical presuppositions informing it are further elaborated in chapter 1. Past efforts at understanding Jesus from a psychological point of view are reviewed and critiqued in an essay on this subject in the Appendix. In chapters 2, 3, and 4, a perspective on the period of Jesus' life leading up to his baptism begins to take shape, one that is then tested and elaborated in chapters 5, 6, 7, and 8. In chapter 9 the most compelling features of the emerging portrait are briefly summarized and assessed as to their possible significance for our time.

I claim no more for this study than that the attempt as such is valid, and that facets of the picture of Jesus that have emerged may be of importance for the construction of a meaningful contemporary christology. "Jesus is a much underrated man," wrote the South African theologian Albert Nolan at the conclusion of his provocative study, *Jesus before Christianity*. "To deprive this man of his humanity [as do those who emphasize his divinity only, or those who regard him as nothing more than a teacher of religious truth] is to deprive him of his greatness."[4] My prayer is that the following study might help the reader to gain not only a deepened appreciation of Jesus' humanity but also a fresh sense of some of the reasons for his abiding greatness and relevance.

The research for this book was begun upon my return to biblical studies following a decade of employment in the field of psychiatric rehabilitation. Many individuals have contributed to its improvement. William Klassen and his wife Donna Harvey were especially insistent that the manuscript should be published. In the fall of 1996 Bill persuaded me to bring it to the attention of Cynthia Thompson of Fortress Press, who in turn sent it to Professor Wayne Rollins for assessment. It was their enthusiasm and helpful comments that brought this project to fruition. There is another person whose unwavering support of this endeavor has kept it alive, my wife Louise. Its dedication to her is a small sign of the admiration, gratitude, and love I have felt for her since first coming to know her half a century ago. "She is beyond the price of pearls. Her husband's heart has confidence in her." She has brought me only "good and not harm" all the days of my life (Pro. 31:10-12, NJB).

1

Introduction

To feel the overwhelming mystery of the incarnation in our time, it is necessary to pass from the initial stage in which we find ourselves, where Jesus is culture hero, through an intermediate stage, in which he becomes fully and unequivocally human for us. . . . To reach this intermediate state . . . we must pass over from the standpoint in which we are subjective and Jesus is objective (as culture hero) to the standpoint in which he is subjective.[1]

Motives

It is understandable if Christians especially, but others as well, should find a psychohistorical study of Jesus initially unsettling. In broaching a subject of this nature, roles are seemingly reversed. Instead of his eyes searching and probing us, ours are probing him. Even to suggest such a possibility is difficult—to pursue it, almost unthinkable. Nevertheless, the "unthinkable" has been thought, and since the beginning of this century there has been a steady stream of studies approaching the life of Jesus from an explicitly psychological point of view, some of them with conclusions that are far from positive.[2] While it is true that such studies and the debates generated by them have, to date, touched only a small segment of the population, there is reason to believe they will soon reach a wider audience. The challenge to think about Jesus in psychological categories is growing, and for two reasons above all: (1) the ascendancy in our time of "historical Jesus" study and (2) the growth of the personality sciences. Although I will be referring to these fields of study repeatedly in other contexts, a few words here may help to orient us to their nature and relevance for the subject at hand.

"Historical Jesus" study is that discipline, now some two centuries old, which seeks to identify in the traditions about Jesus those that most accurately reflect his actual life and teaching. The need for such an approach arose with the awareness that the Gospel accounts of the life of Jesus were significantly shaped by the church that transmitted and collected them.[3] The historian who seeks to distinguish in these sources between the contribution of Jesus and the contribution of the transmitting community must work with probabilities. Historical knowledge (all knowledge, in fact) is approximate and personal. The observer impinges upon the field of knowledge. Admittedly, therefore, the Jesus of history is always, to a degree, the historian's Jesus. Nevertheless, acknowledged results have been achieved, and images of the Jesus of history have begun to emerge that are making an increasingly significant impact on Christian thought and human consciousness generally.[4]

One major effect of this development is the now growing awareness among Christians and non-Christians alike of the *humanity* of Jesus.[5] Confronted by the particularities of the Jesus of history, traditional stereotypes give way to a uniquely individual configuration. This development is amply demonstrated in the survey of modern psychological studies of Jesus in the Appendix, where it can be seen that the very advent of historical Jesus study in and of itself confronts us with a challenge to think about Jesus in a more personal and subjective manner.

This challenge was made all the more inescapable by the ascendancy in this century of the personality sciences and, I might add, developmental psychology in particular. By this latter I refer to that now considerable body of knowledge that has been accumulating since Freud concerning the stages and crises through which human beings must inevitably grow if they are to become mature adults. This data, perhaps best summarized in Erik Erikson's programmatic essays, is gradually revolutionizing our understanding of human subjectivity.[6] For one thing, we now realize, as never before, that the child is in truth "father of the man." We become what we are, emotionally, intellectually, morally, even spiritually, not by sheer willfulness or obstinacy, but by living through a sequence of complex biological, personal, and interpersonal developments, beginning in the very first months of our lives.

These themes have become omnipresent in our culture, and as an inevitable consequence they enter the picture when one looks at Jesus—in any case, when one considers the Jesus of history.[7] Just as it is no longer possible, in our time, to read the Gospels without an increasingly acute awareness of the historicity and humanity of Jesus, it is likewise no longer possible to read them without attention to the personal developmental dynamics of the one who meets us there.

Proof of this trend, were any needed, is the surfacing, in recent books about Jesus, of a host of questions and suggestions virtually ignored by previous generations. "Was Jesus married?" William Phipps has asked in two carefully researched works.[8] "If not, why not?" other authors query.[9] Still others allude to his "egocentricity" and wonder about the impact his exceptional self-identity might have had on his contemporaries.[10] Another hypothesizes that Jesus' alienation from his family might have been the "psychological fact" behind his decision to leave his home in Nazareth and begin his mission,[11] and yet another asks whether his emotional way of addressing God as Abba (father) may not have been the "grand illusion" of his life.[12] "Do we know anything at all about Jesus' developmental experiences as a child or teenager?" others ask. "Once we agree," writes Gerald O'Collins, "that as a genuine human being Jesus developed psychologically, we cannot then ignore Freud, Jung and Erikson by refusing even to raise the question: what could that development have been like—before and after puberty?"[13] Was the adult Jesus emotionally mature? Uniquely mature? Perhaps the sanest and wisest man who ever lived? Or, in his case too, as with the rest of us, were there weaknesses, disorders, temptations that had to be faced and surmounted, perhaps serious ones?[14]

Questions of this nature cannot be suppressed. They are as inevitable in the context of the intellectual climate of our age as were the christological issues so vigorously debated in the first three centuries of Christian history. In fact, they may be in some respects the same issues in a new guise, with only the constructs and vocabulary changed slightly (psychology replacing philosophy as the principal intellectual paradigm).[15] And once articulated, they demand an answer. From the beginning Jesus was experienced as someone about whom it was difficult to remain neutral. People were either for him or against him. It is not surprising, therefore, if those of us today who are "for him" feel anxious when doubts arise regarding him. We can no more rest content with vague, halfhearted responses than could Christians of earlier generations when faced by analogous challenges. Too much is at stake personally, morally, religiously.

Presuppositions

But granted their importance, how are we to go about dealing with questions and themes of this nature? I have already alluded to the approach I will be taking, but a few additional comments may be necessary to make explicit the presuppositions that undergird the following study.

It should be emphasized again, first of all, that it is the psychological profile of the *historical* Jesus that I will be investigating. In focusing the inquiry in this manner, I am not unmindful of the alternatives. Although Jesus was initially the "Jesus of history," his life (as Christians view it) did not end there. After his resurrection he lived again as a transcendent figure for those who believed in him. A new constellation of images and pictures arose to explain who he was and is and the cosmic significance of his life, death, and resurrection. These were at first radically informed by the recollections of those who had been with him "from the baptism of John until the day when he was taken up" (Acts 1:22). But in the course of time the historical memories became weaker and the post-resurrection images took on a life of their own. It was this shift in part that prompted the writing of the earliest Gospels. Christians soon realized that without a picture of Jesus anchored in the actualities of his historical mission, it could become vulnerable to "every wind of doctrine," a plaything of human imagination.[16] A similar insight and instinct motivate contemporary historical Jesus research. In the following study, I too will be holding the more traditional images of Jesus in abeyance, not necessarily because they are outmoded, but so that whatever truth is emerging from the historian's workshop might continue to inform, enrich, anchor, and, if necessary, correct our picture of him.[17]

In pursuing this "quest of the historical Jesus," I will also be relying on the generally accepted methods and results of the research to date. I have already alluded to the fact that our major sources for such a quest, the canonical Gospels, are viewed by modern historians as the end result of the passage of the data about Jesus (what he said and did) through a complex oral and redactional matrix within the milieu of early Christianity. As a result, historical memories and the theology of the transmitting communities (the early Christian, Jewish, and gentile churches) have become intertwined in these documents to a degree that is often difficult to unravel. Methods and criteria for doing so have been identified, however, and can be usefully implemented from case to case.[18] Where, for example, the Synoptics (Matthew, Mark, Luke) share traditions in common, it is now generally thought that Mark is the older, more primary source for the other two. It is also widely hypothesized that sayings and episodes common only to Matthew and Luke (but not in Mark) also derive from an earlier source (frequently referred to as "Q"). It does not follow, of course, that Mark and Q are uniformly more historical, only that they bring us one step closer to the historical starting point. On the other hand, information about Jesus in any of our sources that is in tension with well-known theological tendencies of the early Christian churches may well be historically authentic, for otherwise, why would the transmitting communities feel constrained to retain it? In addition there is the well-established presumption in favor of the historicity of episodes and teachings that are strikingly original when viewed against Jesus' immediate Jewish background (without denying, of course, that Jesus was also a child of his time and as such held many ideas in common with his Jewish contemporaries). It may also be noted that information verified by several independent sources (Mark, Q, special-Luke, special-Matthew, John) and forms (parables, sayings, stories) may likewise be viewed as having a heightened historical probability on its side.

This does not mean that only data that passes the test of these criteria can be assigned to the "historical Jesus." The reasons are sometimes varied and subtle for evaluating one facet of the tradition and not another as a more authentic feature of the portrait of the Jesus of history.[19] In general, in the study that follows I will be relying on the more substantial conclusions of the recognized historians at work in the field.[20]

The same holds true for the psychological point of view that I will bring to bear on the subject at hand—the major goal of our inquiry. It is well known that psychology is one of the youngest and most subjective of the major scientific disciplines and, consequently, still conflict-ridden to an exceptional degree. It might seem, therefore, that any attempt to approach the life of Jesus from this standpoint is premature and jeopardized from the start. In reality, however, only a very few recognized schools of psychology profess to tell us in any detail how human personality in all its complexity develops from childhood onward. And only one of these has thus far not only survived empirical testing but demonstrated a remarkable capacity for interacting with historical disciplines in fruitful ways. This is the already mentioned developmental point of view pioneered by Freud and elaborated by neo-Freudians like Fromm, Erikson, Levinson, and others.[21] Here, in contrast to earlier psychological approaches, the emphasis falls on an awareness of carefully identified epigenetic stages (one stage building on another from birth through adulthood) during which phase-specific emotional-moral challenges must be faced and surmounted for optimal ongoing well-being. Especially important for the following study are Freud's insights into the dynamics of the so-called oedipal period from three to six, as well as Erikson's and Levinson's analysis of adult life stages—the so-called "Age Thirty Transition" in particular.[22]

In summary, I have tried to point out in this opening chapter that historical study and psychology are converging in our culture to create a significant new matrix for understanding Jesus. As a result, when reading the Gospels we inevitably begin thinking of him as possessing a humanity and subjectivity as complex and dynamic as we now know our own to be. If Jesus is to continue to occupy a place among us as guide, savior, mediator, prototype, we are thus compelled to form a clearer, more intelligent impression of this side of his life than may have seemed necessary in previous generations. Such an investigation is especially important in the light of the questions about Jesus' psyche that have already been raised, some of them negative in the extreme (see the Appendix for a survey of psychological studies of Jesus). A historically disciplined approach to the Gospels together with the insights of contemporary developmental psychology would seem to offer the most promising basis for pressing forward in this urgent task.

2 The Starting Point

Nietzsche was right when he wrote: "All the attempts I know of to construct the history of a 'soul' from the Gospels seem to me to imply a deplorable levity in psychological matters." There is, however, a psychological element in the life of Jesus that we may not ignore: his rejection of the family into which he was born.[1]

His Family

In taking a fresh psychohistorical look at the Jesus of history, there is little question about where to begin. If psychology since Freud has taught us anything, it is the way early experiences in the immediate family shape our emotional outlook. If we hope to get a firmer hold on the idiosyncrasies of the adult Jesus' inner world, it is to those texts that reflect his experience of father, mother, brothers, and sisters that we must turn first of all.

In attempting to do so, however, there are major difficulties to surmount in identifying the relevant texts to be studied and how to understand them. To marshall the many-sided data of history and psychology that seem relevant to an inquiry of this kind is a delicate task. Another factor to be reckoned with in the abrupt rejection that psychohistorical inquiries have sometimes received is simply our emotional resistance to the kind of materials on which psychologists tend to focus. But just as important may be the sheer complexity of it all.

Complexity of course arises not only in trying to understand someone in the past whose life-record is not especially full or clear. Therapists are often baffled by the "story" of the client right in front of them. While patterns do recur, every individual is mysteriously unique, and a given account may look at first like a jungle of contradictions. The therapist strains to understand but cannot. If at last light begins to shine, the insight may come in connection with some seemingly inconsequential yet strangely emotion-packed memory, incident, or dream. For a biography in the traditional sense it might have little or no importance, but client and therapist know that they have stumbled onto a piece of psychic reality. There in that surcharged recollection, in that fragment of fantasy, a window begins to open into the inner world of this particular life. More often than not it has to do with primal human relationships.

This experience so common in psychotherapeutic practice may help to explain why, in trying to interpret the biographies of "great" men and women, psychohistorians so often focus on what might appear at first sight to be only a triviality. Thus Freud, for example, in his famous study of Leonardo da Vinci, abruptly introduces us to a "cradle memory" about a suffocating vulture (or kite) attack that Leonardo recorded off the cuff, so to speak, in one of his journals.[2] Behind that childhood fantasy Freud thought he glimpsed a formative experience with Leonardo's unmarried mother from whose arms he was taken, sometime before his fifth year, to join his father's household.

Erik Erikson began his Luther study in similar fashion by relating the episode of the great reformer's "fit in the choir," where Luther suddenly shouted before a startled congregation, "Ich bin's nit! Ich bin's nit!" ("It's not me! It's not me!").[3] Erikson writes that this scene kept coming back to him as he pondered the data of young Luther's life and tried to understand its inner workings. Only as Luther was able to break free of the negative self-image born of his relation to his human father ("It's not me!") could he begin to make that transition to "faith" in God (his spiritual father) that was to form the core of his later identity and vocation.

In pursuing our inquiry into Jesus' psyche at thirty, it is worth asking: Does anything of this nature come to our attention here? The material accessible to us for studying the life of Jesus has, of course, been open to public scrutiny for centuries and examined from virtually every angle.

The likelihood of our coming across revelations of a kind that would suddenly shed vast new light on Jesus' psychological development would appear, therefore, to be very remote indeed.

Estrangement

It was suggested above that psychology has taught us that if we wish to lay hold of the emotional configuration of a given individual's life, we must pay especially close attention to any data at all that might give evidence of unique familial dynamics, even if, at first glance, such data would appear to be of little or no interest to a biography in the traditional sense. And there does happen to be in the Gospels at least one sometimes neglected item of this nature: the account in Mark 3:19b-21 of a rather shocking action on the part of Jesus' family shortly after the beginning of his public mission. It should be kept in mind that Jesus' base of operations during this phase of his activity was Capernaum, a fishing village on the northwest rim of the Sea of Galilee some twenty-five miles from Nazareth where he grew up. The verses referred to may be translated with reasonable certainty as follows:

> Then he [Jesus] went home [to Capernaum]; and the crowd came together again, so that they [Jesus and his disciples] could not even eat. And when those close to him [his immediate family] heard it, they went out [from Nazareth] to seize him, for they said, "He is beside himself."[4]

It is worth pausing a moment to consider what a strange fate this brief but rather unsettling bit of information has suffered in Gospel studies. Not only was it rather quickly extinguished in all canonical traditions save one (Mark's Gospel), but it is even today largely ignored by Christian scholars. One cannot help noticing a striking contrast at this point on the part of modern Jewish scholarship. Whereas Bornkamm, Dodd, Trocmé, and Jeremias, for example (all Protestants), virtually bypass this text in their comprehensive reviews of Jesus' life and teachings, its existence and bearing on the larger question of Jesus' relation to his family are both acknowledged and explored in the works of Klausner, Flusser, and Vermes (all Jewish).[5] Since the information is obviously there, one can hardly fault the Jewish scholars for noting it (and especially not when they treat it in the restrained and sympathetic way they do). What raises questions is the silence on the part of the Christians. This silence, of course, is not deliberate but symptomatic rather of a still widespread and largely unconscious resistance to a full recognition of Jesus' humanity and the more obvious emotional factors at work within it.

Neither the substance nor the historicity of what these verses relate seems to be in serious doubt. While the language is Mark's, writes Vincent Taylor, "without the warrant of fact no early narrator would have alleged that the family of Nazareth thought that Jesus was beside Himself and went out to restrain him."[6] At the very least what this passage suggests is that, for whatever reasons, an estrangement had opened up between Jesus and his family at this juncture of his life—an estrangement so deep that communication had completely broken down between them.

Other Gospel passages also hint at this state of affairs. We are told, for example, of only one visit by Jesus to his home in Nazareth during his entire public mission. But even this visit, it turned out, was an abortive one (Matt. 13:54-58//Mark 6:1-6a//Luke 4:16-30), for the emotional atmosphere on that occasion, it is reported, was so hostile that Jesus was powerless to do there what he did elsewhere (Mark 6:5). The pathos of this unexpected development is summed up by a single sentence in John's Gospel: "He came to his own home, and his own people received him not" (John 1:11). There too it is explicitly stated that Jesus' own brothers were among those who "did not believe in him" (John 7:5).

The depth of this estrangement is also revealed in the episode described in Mark 3:31-35 (Matt. 12:46-50//Luke 8:19-21), where Jesus' mother and brothers are portrayed in the very act of visiting Capernaum, ostensibly to implement the plan referred to in Mark 3:19b-21 ("they went out to seize him, for they said, 'He is beside himself'"). When, however, they arrived at the place where Jesus was teaching, a crowd surrounded him. All that was possible was to send him a message: "Your mother and your brothers are outside, asking for you" (Mark 3:32). When Jesus heard of it, Mark informs us, his response was a surprising one. "Respect for his mother," comments Joseph Klausner, "(a prominent trait among the Jews, ranked in the Ten Commandments on the same level as respect for the father) required that he should go to her at once."[7] Instead, he said: "Who are my mother and my brothers?" And then "looking around on those who sat about him," he exclaimed, "Here are my mother and my brothers! Whoever does the will of God is my brother, and sister, and mother."

Although these passages do not tell us much, they do highlight the tensions that seem to have characterized the relations of Jesus and his family during this phase of his life. It is Luke who informs us that Jesus was "about thirty" at this time (Luke 3:23).[8] This pertinent bit of information only intensifies our astonishment that Jesus' family appears to be so utterly baffled and offended by his behavior, and that Jesus on his part is so totally aloof.[9] For the sake of a spiritual family, it seems, this now fully adult Jesus will not give an inch to his biological family—no direct word of response to their request to see him, not even the slightest gesture of conciliation. Pondering this scene, one thinks of the story of how Gautama Buddha one day at about the same age in life abruptly turned his back on his parental home (and in that instance, on wife and child as well), to seek and then teach a new way to a growing circle of disciples.

We are also reminded by all this of Jesus' sayings about the priority of doing God's will over family ties, sayings that run like a refrain through his recorded teachings. Do not these statements also hint at and reflect, in some sense, Jesus' own personal estrangement from his family of origin? In one of them, for example, he speaks of those who have "left house or brothers or parents or children, for the sake of the kingdom of God" (Luke 18:29b-30). Is this not what Jesus himself is portrayed as doing in the scenes we have just looked at? Or when a would-be follower approached him with the request that he first be allowed "to go and bury my father" (Luke 9:60//Matt. 8:22), is it not possible that his reply was as abrupt as it was ("leave the dead to bury their dead") because he too had faced a similar conflict?[10] On another occasion, an anonymous woman is reported to have shouted from the crowds a blessing on his mother: "Blessed is the womb that bore you and the breasts that you sucked" (Luke 11:27). There was no need to respond. But we are told that he rebuked her with words similar to those he had used earlier in distancing himself from the mother herself: "Blessed rather are those who hear the word of God and keep it" (Luke 11:28). Even if it is true that the statement in Luke 14:26 about "hating father and mother and wife and children and brothers and sisters" (if one wishes to be a disciple) is hyperbole, it is again the same intrafamilial conflict that surfaces.

"Do you think that I have come to give peace on earth? No, I tell you, but rather division; for henceforth in one house there will be five divided, three against two, and two against three . . ." (Luke 12:51f.). ". . . A man's foes will be those of his own household" (Matt. 10:36).

Only too obviously, Jesus saw life's ultimate loyalties as potentially discordant with the claims of biological family. By alluding to the tensions that existed between Jesus and his own family, the Gospels intimate that this way of looking at reality may have been rooted in the depths of Jesus' own experience with his own "mother and brothers and sisters."

The Traditional Portrait

What are we to make of these family tensions, psychologically? To say the least, a rupture of this magnitude in the relationship of the "about thirty"-year-old Jesus and his family must pose serious questions for the portrait traditionally drawn of his personal and emotional development and his transition to public life. Typically, that portrait accents a steady evolution of consciousness from birth to public Messiahship, an evolution in which the entire family is generally thought to have participated. This portrait, to be sure, also has its roots in the Gospel traditions, taking its clues above all from the Matthean and Lukan infancy narratives in which Jesus' identity and destiny are known (to the parents at least) from conception onward. On this basis it can be imagined that Jesus himself learned at an early age of his approaching role in the divine plan, "increased in wisdom and in stature, and in favor with God and man" (Luke 2:52), and (together with parents and siblings) quietly awaited the moment when he would be revealed to the world.

> It seems to me that it is reasonable to think that from the moment when He was found among the Doctors, and especially once an adult, Jesus revealed progressively to Joseph and Mary absolutely all the mysteries of God which he had come in order to announce. In view of their immense mutual love, how would He have been able not to communicate to them, to them first, that which He was to communicate to the apostles and to all men?

This is the picture of Jesus and his family drawn by the French Catholic philosopher Jacques Maritain in one of his last books.[11] But it simply fragments in the light of the knowledge that precisely at the moment when Jesus did step forward to "communicate to the apostles and to all men," a deep gulf opened up between himself and his family—a gulf that apparently was not rectified until the post-resurrection period (Acts 1:14).[12]

An Alternative

If the traditional view is inadequate and unacceptable, how then *are* we to account for Jesus' estrangement at thirty from precisely those individuals with whom we might anticipate he would have had the closest rapport: the members of his immediate family? The texts looked at thus far suggest only the very beginnings of an answer to this crucial question. It will require the remaining chapters of this study to answer it more completely. However, certain important clues have already emerged.

It is evident, first of all, that the alienation hinted at in the data just reviewed was the result of changes and initiatives on *Jesus'* part, not his family's. He is the one who shattered the expectations and stereotypes to the point where they were forced to conclude he was "beside himself." Furthermore, our sources imply that whatever it was that had happened in Jesus' life to bring about these changes happened suddenly—so suddenly that both family and neighbors were caught off guard. "Where did this man get all this. . . . Is not this the carpenter, the son of Mary and brother of James and Joses and Judas and Simon, and are not his sisters here with us?" (Mark 6:2-3).

Finally, the account of Jesus' response to the visit of his family to the scene of his public mission at Capernaum (Mark 3:31-35), taken together with his sayings about the absolute priority of doing God's will over family ties, intimates that the gulf that had opened between them at this time was largely the consequence of substantive *inner* changes on his part. From being an obscure member of an artisan family living in an insignificant Galilean village, he appears to have emerged (with a suddenness and boldness that startled and alienated family and neighbors) a forceful, much-sought-after "evangelist" with a passionate sense of doing God's will (Mark 3:35).

Is there any confirmation of this picture elsewhere in our sources? If so, is there any evidence that might explain what, more precisely, happened to Jesus at this juncture of his life to bring about such a striking transformation?

3 The Turning Point

There are many things that have been thought to set Jesus apart from other men and have seemed to establish a gulf: his Christhood, his sinlessness, his miraculous power, his divinity. I wonder, for my own part, if it is not rather his conversion. . . . It is sometimes said that Jesus sanctified the ordinary ways of mankind by living a retiring and unnoticed life for so many years in a small village. Did he sanctify them or did he leave them behind when the light finally dawned?[1]

Baptism

The canonical sources for the life of Jesus leave us in no doubt as to where to look for the answer to the question concerning what may have precipitated the break between Jesus and his family. They point with one accord to his encounter with one of the "great men" of his generation, John the Baptist. It is this encounter, these Gospels tell us, that marked the transition from Jesus' "hidden years" to his public ministry. In fact, it is almost as though with this event Jesus came fully alive for the first time. From birth to thirty, the life of Jesus is virtually a blank. It is first through his meeting with John the Baptist that he entered upon that way of life that so shocked his family and was eventually to disquiet the world.

It all happened, we are told, in the days when this John was preaching repentance and baptizing at the Jordan with crowds streaming to him from all Judea. It was then that Jesus also left his home to join them and was himself baptized (Mark 1:9-11). But even more important, this was the occasion, our earliest sources tell us, when Jesus had an experience that they intimate was decisive for all that was to follow. Immediately after his baptism (Mark 1:10), while praying (Luke 3:21), he saw the heavens open, experienced the Spirit descending dove-like upon him, and heard a voice saying: "Thou art my beloved son; with you I am well pleased" (Mark 1:11).[2]

That Jesus was in fact baptized by John the Baptist is historically unquestionable, for the memory of this event hinted at a subordination of Jesus to John and a need on Jesus' part for repentance and forgiveness that was wholly at variance with the developing christology of the early church. "Such a scandalizing piece of information cannot have been invented."[3]

Doubts have been raised, however, about the historicity of the "vision" that Jesus is said to have had on this occasion. If Jesus did have such an experience at this juncture of his life, he alone would have known of it, initially. Others would have learned of it only if he told them. We need to ask, therefore, whether it is at all plausible that Jesus did in fact have such a visionary experience, and if he did, whether there would have been any compelling reason for relating it to anyone else.

Three respected biblical scholars, Joachim Jeremias, James Dunn, and J. Ramsey Michaels, in substantial studies have answered yes to both of these questions.[4] Dunn, for example, calls our attention to the fact that the earliest account of Jesus' experience at his baptism (in Mark) emphasizes that this was the occasion on which two things happened to Jesus: (1) he received the Spirit (2) and he became conscious that he was God's son. It is virtually certain, Dunn writes, that Jesus began his public mission profoundly conscious of precisely these two realities (Spirit and sonship). Convictions of this nature, he adds, "must have crystallized at some point in his life. Why [then] should the traditions unanimously fasten on this episode in Jesus' life [as the time when this happened] if they had no reason for making the link and many reasons against it?"[5]

Equally important in assessing the historicity of this experience is the fact that subsequent to his baptism, during his public mission, Jesus thought of himself as a prophet (Mark 6:4; Luke 13:33).[6] It is well known, however, that a man is not born a prophet, but *becomes* one through a shattering divine call. If, then, Jesus was self-consciously prophetic, he too must have had such a call. For the prophets generally, call experiences of this nature were so important that almost inevitably the time came when they had to speak of them either to their disciples or their critics, in defense and explanation of their prophetic calling (Amos 7:10-17; Hos. 1:2; Isa. 6; Jer. 1:4-10). That Jesus too, on occasion, may have spoken of his baptism in this manner (and for this reason) is not simply a matter of conjecture. At least two Gospel passages have frequently been cited as possibly alluding to Jesus' baptismal vision, and in a manner that highlights the great importance this experience must have had for him. One such text is the cryptic word in Matthew11:27 (Luke 10:22), the opening line of which can be translated: "A full revelation has been given me by my father. . . ." Jeremias has argued that this ecstatic utterance, spoken by Jesus at a critical moment in mid-career when opposition was rising against him, is a direct reference to the words he heard at his baptism. In other words, the audition, "You are my beloved son . . . ," Jeremias believes, had revelatory significance for Jesus.[7]

Again, during his final week in Jerusalem, when challenged by his critics to give an account of his authority for doing the audacious things he did there, Jesus is said to have responded by asking in return: "Was the baptism of John from heaven or from men? Answer me" (Mark 11:30). This question too, it has been suggested, was not just a ploy—a diversionary tactic, so to speak—but a serious counterchallenge that further verifies the vital link that Jesus felt to exist between John and himself. For Jesus, the "baptism of John" and what he himself had experienced with John at the Jordan were unquestionably "from heaven" and foundational for his entire mission.[8]

In summary, "the case is hardly proved," writes Dunn, "but we may say with some confidence that . . . *Jesus' baptism by John was probably the occasion for an experience of God which had epochal significance for Jesus. . . .*"[9]

What Really Happened?

But what, more precisely, happened to Jesus on this occasion? We must proceed cautiously. Data relevant to an understanding of Jesus' baptismal experience will be slowly accumulating throughout the remaining chapters of this study. My comments at this stage should be viewed as no more than an initial exploratory "reading" of the baptismal texts themselves, especially the record of this event in Mark, our earliest source.

It has already been noted that Mark 1:11 alludes to a disclosure experience involving not one but two events: a vision of the opening of the heavens and the dove-like descent of the Spirit; and an audition, literally translated: "You are my Son, the beloved, with you I am well pleased." Is it possible, to begin with, that the first of these (the "descent of the Spirit") is intended to refer to an inner subjective experience on Jesus' part? It is well known, in any case, that among the Jews the Spirit-filled person was thought of as someone inwardly empowered (Acts 1:8). That the text speaks of the Spirit descending "like a dove" (not "in bodily form *as* a dove," as Luke 3:22 too literally reinterprets it) could then be suggestive of the gentle quality of this experience. Jesus, on this occasion, experienced a gentle quickening power within. But how, were this the case, should we understand the accompanying audition ("Thou art my Son . . .")? Dunn proposes that the more precise nature of the "spiritual" experience that Jesus had on this occasion is made explicit in the *words* that he heard.[10] Spirit and audition point to overlapping realities. In other words, what descended upon Jesus in this moment of his life was the gentle empowering experience of "sonship."

But the notion of sonship also requires elucidation. Sonship in what sense? Until recently it was simply assumed that Jesus' baptism marked either the beginning or the confirmation of Jesus' sense of *messianic* sonship. The words "Thou art my son . . . ," it was thought, were tantamount to saying, "You are the Messiah!" But this assumption is now clouded by the realization that "son of God" was not the way the great majority of Palestinian Jews in that period thought of this devoutly hoped-for deliverer.[11] The early Christians, of course, thought differently. We are compelled to look elsewhere, however, if we wish to understand the meaning that the words "beloved son" might have had for Jesus.

Scriptural allusions are sometimes cited as having had a bearing on this question. The opening phrase of Jesus' baptismal audition ("Thou art my Son . . .") sounds very much like the enthronement decree in Psalm 2:7 (literally, "My son you . . ."), and the closing phrase of the audition (". . . the beloved, with you I am well pleased") reminds us of the words in Isaiah 42:1 addressed to God's servant (". . . my chosen, in whom my soul delights"). However, the verbal similarities are by no means exact, and the issue is unresolved as to which of these two scriptural passages might be paramount as a context for interpreting these words, or if in fact an altogether different context should be sought.[12] Perhaps then the audition is not really a quotation from anywhere, but carried significance uniquely personal to Jesus.

A quite different background factor may therefore be of some significance. Several contemporary Jewish scholars have pointed to the possible importance of a hitherto unnoticed *charismatic* element in the Judaism of Jesus' day for an understanding of his spiritual milieu generally and his experience of sonship in particular.[13] Exemplary figures of this tradition, men like Honi the Circle Drawer and the Galilean Hanina ben Dosa, are described in the Mishnah as having cast out demons, wrought miracles through prayer, and related to God in other ways reminiscent of scenes in the Gospels. In addition, these men are reported to have thought of themselves, in some special sense, as "sons" of God. Honi, for example, once prayed: "Lord of the universe, thy sons have turned to me because I am as a *son of the house* before thee."[14] Is this, then, what "sonship" might have meant for Jesus also? When the "voice" singled him out at his baptism as "beloved son," did he too experience this "naming" as a gift of divine acceptance and rapport analogous to that of other charismatics of his generation?

This possibility points to yet another. As noted, the words Jesus heard at the time of his baptism cannot readily be identified as a direct quotation from anywhere. Nor can they be readily stereotyped as messianic. If anything, as we have just seen, a charismatic background may be postulated. But charismatic experience is notoriously individual and personal. These observations all suggest that what transpired within Jesus on this occasion was unique and without any fixed or precise prototypes.

Among contemporary scholars it is Dunn in particular who has sensed this possibility and explored it in a wide-ranging, systematic manner. His remarkable conclusions as to the meaning that sonship had for Jesus generally are as follows:

> Jesus' sense of being God's son was an existential *conviction* [he writes], not merely an intellectual belief. He *experienced* a relation of sonship—felt such an intimacy with God, such an approval by

> God, dependence on God, responsibility to God, that the only words adequate to express it were "Father" and "Son." . . . The point is that basic to Jesus' self-consciousness and consciousness of mission was not any particular messianic title or OT concept to which he then added the concept "Son of God." The evidence indicates rather that Jesus' sense of sonship was primary..[15]

Dunn rightly goes on to emphasize that appreciation of this uniquely personal dimension of Jesus' core religious experience is a much neglected element in contemporary historical Jesus study.

The Psychological Matrix

It is a little surprising, therefore, that having written so persuasively on this subject, Dunn should go on to repeat the opinion so often found in modern Jesus studies, namely, that ". . . the evidence certainly does not permit us to trace a psychological development in Jesus."[16] If this statement means that we lack the evidence for reconstructing as full or detailed an account in this regard as we might wish, then Dunn is of course correct. If, however, it is implied that the available data does not permit us to say anything at all about the personal factors that might have impinged on Jesus' baptismal experience in particular and his adult life generally, then this conclusion is just as obviously misleading. The Gospels themselves only too clearly indicate that what happened to Jesus at this time of his life did not occur in a vacuum. There were personal antecedents to his baptismal vision, they intimate, some of which lie chronologically close at hand, others of which can be deduced from what we are told elsewhere in the Gospels about Jesus' life generally prior to and after this event. In trying to understand an experience of this nature, it can also be helpful to draw upon comparable experiences in the lives of others as well as the established results of religious and developmental psychology.

So far as antecedents "chronologically close at hand" are concerned, it is apparent, to begin with, that the personality and message of John the Baptist himself must have had a catalytic effect on what occurred within Jesus on this occasion. All of Jesus' sayings about John suggest that his identification with this awesome figure was profound. John was a prophet, yes, more than a prophet (Matt. 11:9//Luke 7:26). He was someone to be "believed" in. "For John came to you in the way of righteousness and you did not believe him," Jesus once charged the religious elite (Matt. 21:32), "but the tax collectors and the harlots believed him; and even when you saw it, you did not afterward repent and believe him." With John, Jesus declared, a new historical epoch had dawned (Matt. 11:12b). He was the greatest man who ever lived (Matt. 11:11).[17]

"What did you go out in the wilderness to see?" Jesus one time queried those who (like him) had been with John at the Jordan (Matt. 11:7). The words of Jesus about John just cited, taken in conjunction with the portrait of John in our oldest sources, begin to clarify what *Jesus himself*, in any case, went out to see. John's message was shocking. Israel, John believed, stood on the brink of disaster (Matt. 3:10//Luke 3:9). The ax was already laid to the root of the tree. Being children of Abraham in and of itself was no guarantee of salvation, for according to him a mighty messianic figure stood in the wings, winnowing fork already in hand to clear the threshing floor of chaff and to gather the wheat into his granary (Matt. 3:12//Luke 3:17). Only those who repented and were baptized and who bore fruit that befits repentance could hope to escape the wrath to come (Mark 1:4; Matt. 3:7f.//Luke 3:7f.).

This mighty summons to repentance was directed by John to the entire Jewish population regardless of social or moral circumstances or sectarian affiliation. From John's point of view, writes Ben Meyer, "there was no time, no need, no place for long study of the Torah, for priestly robes, for isolation in *elite* groups, for a massively detailed *halaka* to guide the conduct of life." John's mission was "strikingly independent" of the "separatist stance generated by the Pharisees' condemnation of the unobservant" in that it "was addressed to all as a possibility for all."[18] For this very reason, however, those associated with the Jewish religious establishment rejected John's message (Luke 7:29-35; Matt. 21:32), for if what John was saying were true, then *all* would be guilty and in need of divine forgiveness—even they. Even worse, John's proclamation implied that *anyone* could find God's forgiveness, no matter how sinful, simply on the basis of a single act of penitence and water baptism (Mark 1:4). For the Jewish Torah-loyal groups in charge of temple and synagogue (the Sadducees and Pharisees), such an orientation must have bordered on heresy, for it seemingly by-passed their own carefully worked out procedures and norms for affiliating with God's holy people.

For many others, however, John's proclamation was enormously attractive. These were the "harlots, tax-collectors, and sinners" (Matt. 21:32f.; Luke 7:29-35), and the masses of Torah-lax commoners ("people of the land," as they are referred to in talmudic sources—that multitude of "sheep without a shepherd" (Matt. 9:36) who figure so prominently in the Gospel accounts of both John's and Jesus' missions.[19] For them John's baptism opened wide a door to God and to religious identity that they must have thought was forever closed to them. Small wonder that the "good news" (Luke 3:18) of John's mission drew them en masse out of their towns and villages to the Jordan where he preached and baptized (Mark 1:5).

That Jesus joined those alienated masses in their trek to John, as our sources tell us he did, would suggest that he, too, at this time of his life, was one of them and was searching for religious alternatives—that he, too, was moved by John's fiery call to repentance and the promise of forgiveness of sins through baptism. Christian theology has shied away from conclusions of this nature. Already Matthew's Gospel sought to correct the impression left by Mark that Jesus underwent baptism for personal needs of his own. "John would have prevented him," writes Matthew (3:14), but Jesus said, "Let it be so now; for thus it is fitting for us to fulfill all righteousness" (Matt. 3:15).[20] Echoing this traditional point of view, a more recent interpreter has written:

> With certainty Jesus' baptism was not "a baptism of repentance for the remission of sins" (Mark 1:4) so far as his personal life was concerned, for neither on this occasion nor any other does he betray any consciousness of personal sin.[21]

Here once again, however, an otherwise commendable reverence may be in danger of suppressing data essential to a coherent psychohistorical reconstruction. "Consciousness of personal sin" on Jesus' part is by no means as completely absent from the Gospel accounts as the traditional view would suggest. This observation could be made even had we no other evidence than Mark 10:18, where Jesus is reported to have rebuked a would-be disciple for calling him "good," because, he declared, "No one is good but God alone" (himself not excepted). But there is an even more compelling reason, I think, for challenging the historicity of the traditional picture in this respect, and that is the dilemma that would confront us, were that picture true, in knowing how to account for Jesus' insight into the darker aspects of the human heart (Mark 7:14-23//Matt. 15:10-20) and his utterly passionate focus on forgiveness as the epitome of religious experience. Is it conceivable that the world religious leader who above all others attacked self-righteousness and sought to foster humility and awareness of God's grace (Luke 18:9-14), himself had no personal experience of what he was talking about? The traditional insistence that Jesus was "without sin" (or even the consciousness of sin) is understandable as an outgrowth of reverence but corresponds neither to the realities of human experience nor to the earliest testimony of the Gospels.[22]

Mark's account is altogether plausible, therefore, when it implies that Jesus went out to the Jordan for baptism, moved by inner needs of his own. But what, more specifically, might these have been?

Second Birth

Our ability to advance our inquiry at this point will depend in part on the degree to which we are able and willing to look at Jesus' baptismal experience in the light of analogous experiences on the part of others. This would mean, first of all, readiness to draw on relevant observations from a branch of knowledge usually referred to as the psychology of religion. Are there any well-established conclusions from this disciplinary field that might shed further light on what transpired within Jesus at his baptism?

I believe there are. Since the beginning of this century, on the basis of thousands of case histories, students of religious experience have observed that growth into personal and religious maturity generally follows one of two paths (with many variations, of course). There are those who come to religious faith *gradually*, moving from one stage in life to another with few or no emotionally disruptive moments. William James was a pioneer in studies of this kind. In his classic work, *The Varieties of Religious Experience*, he characterized persons of this type as the "once-born," and noted that their adult experience of God and of life corresponds to the more optimistic "healthy-minded" religion (as he termed it) usually to be found in the more liberal groups of a given period.[23] The sociologist Pitrim Sorokin observed the same phenomena in his studies of altruism and classified people of this type as "fortunate altruists."

They "are loving and friendly from childhood," he wrote, and "grow graciously in their love behaviour, without any catastrophic conversion or sharp change in their egos, values, or group membership."[24]

There is a second group, however, for whom the pathway to religious and personal maturity is more difficult. Those in this group typically go through a period of prolonged inner distress, lasting sometimes into adulthood. James called them "sick souls," not meaning thereby to disparage them but only to indicate what they themselves reported of their emotionally chaotic inner world during this time of their lives.[25] Once again, Sorokin noted the same phenomenon and termed people in this category "late catastrophics" or "late altruists," because their breakthrough into altruism often came late in adulthood, after an extended period of emotional turmoil. Both James and Sorokin also observed that for this group to find peace with God and others, a conversion-type experience was required, an emotional reorientation of such magnitude that it could be likened to a "second birth." Prior to this conversion it was as though these persons had hardly begun to live. They were agitated, conflicted, despairing. During the conversion experience itself, they reported encountering God in personal, tangible ways. From it they emerged surrendered, full of joy and a compelling sense of mission.[26]

Do these few elementary observations begin to shed any further light on what might have transpired within Jesus at the time of his baptism? Clearly, this baptism occurred within the context of a "conversionist" movement. This in itself would indicate that the second of the two developmental sketches outlined above is more germane to an understanding of his experience on this occasion. Furthermore, if Jesus underwent some kind of conversion, might he not also have lived through a period of inner conflict before this event, as is typical of those who undergo experiences of this type? When we are told, for example, that immediately following his baptism he had an experience of the Spirit coming upon him and a voice within assured him that he was a son beloved of God and pleasing in God's sight, does this not suggest that in the days, weeks, and months leading up to this event something was missing in this regard?

I will be exploring this and other possibilities associated with this event in the subsequent chapters. What I wish to emphasize now is that the facts considered thus far seem to favor the hypothesis that Jesus belongs to the ranks of those who are compelled to live through a prolonged identity crisis lasting well into adulthood, and who resolve this crisis through a "second birth," as James, Sorokin, and others have described it.[27] Also to be kept in mind are texts considered in chapter 2 that intimate that this crisis, in Jesus' case, might well have orbited around disturbances between himself, his mother, and his siblings. From a psychological point of view this would not be surprising, since psychohistorical research (as already noted) has progressively illuminated the developmental importance of precisely this primary familial matrix.[28] In this light John the Baptist's possible role emerges as a surrogate parent to Jesus in his search for spiritual and vocational integrity. We can say more about this role, however, only when we have gone more deeply into what can be known about the dynamics of Jesus' relationship with his family of origin, and with his father in particular.

4

Jesus and His Father

Fathers, if they know how to hold and guide a child, function somewhat like guardians of the child's autonomous existence. . . . For there is something which only a father can do, which is, I think, to balance the threatening and forbidding aspects of his appearance and impression with the guardianship of the guiding voice. Next to the recognition bestowed by the gracious face, the affirmation of the guiding voice is a prime element of a man's sense of identity.[1]

The Father Problem

Our inquiry thus far has made us increasingly aware of at least two dimensions of Jesus' emotional world at thirty: an alienation from his immediate family and his experience of God as gracious father at the Jordan. This latter, we have suggested, may have been a factor in the former: that is, Jesus' experience of God as gracious father at the time of his baptism seems to have been a major force in the personal transformation that led to his departure from home and the mission that so estranged him from his family. In other words, encountering God as loving father at the Jordan was a disruptive event for Jesus. It set him on a new path.

But as we have already noted, disruptive, disjunctive experiences of this kind do not happen in a vacuum. They are the culmination of sometimes complex social and emotional processes. If, therefore, the reality of God as gracious father broke in upon Jesus at his baptism, then we must imagine that there were developmental problems in the background of this experience having to do with paternal matters generally. Can we say more specifically what these might have been? Do our Gospel sources tell us anything at all, directly or indirectly, about Jesus' paternal experiences in the years before his baptism, experiences that might shed some further light on what happened at the Jordan and subsequently in his public mission?

Hard Data

To pursue our investigation at this point is difficult because of the well-known lack of hard data about the early years of Jesus. Even the few accounts we do have of the circumstances of his birth and childhood (the so-called "infancy narratives" of Matthew 1–2 and Luke 1–2) are now generally regarded as legendary and of very little historical value.[2] It would be wrong to imply, however, that we have no information at all in this respect. There is general agreement that what remains after a critical sifting of the available facts concerning Jesus' childhood, youth, and early adulthood may be outlined roughly as follows:

Name: Yeshua (Aramaic), Joshua (Hebrew), Jesus (Greek).
Date of birth: toward the end of the reign of Herod the Great (4 or 5 B.C.E.; Matt. 2:1).
Home village: Nazareth of Galilee (John 19:19; Luke 1:26).
Father's name: Joseph (Luke 3:23; 4:22; Matt. 1:16; John 1:45; 6:42).[3]
Mother's name: Mary (Hebrew: Miriam; Mark 6:3/Matt. 13:55).
Siblings: James (Jacob), Joses (Joseph), Judas (Judah), Simon, several sisters (Mark 6:3/Matt. 13:55).
Place in family: first-born (Luke 2:7).
Occupation: carpenter (Greek: *Tekton*), as was his father (Mark 6:3; Matt. 13:55).
Religion: Judaism.
Marital status: uncertain.

In reflecting on this data it is important, first of all, that we take full measure of its paucity. The so-called "silent" or "hidden years" of Jesus are truly "hidden"! In fact, the silence is so great that one has to wonder if this might not be a datum in its own right. Why this dearth of information about the greater part of the life of one whose followers soon revered him as the most important figure in human history?

The answer sometimes given is that men and women of that age did not share our interest in the everyday affairs of their great men.[4] This may be true, but we also know that curiosity about Jesus' early life soon became an important factor in Christian piety, resulting in a growing fund of stories about his childhood activities, many of them fantastic.[5] Why, as this interest grew, did the church have so little to say in the face of the absurdities soon propagated in his name, especially if it were true that Jesus' mother and brothers were at one time leading members of that church (Acts 1:14)? A silence so great must mean something. One conclusion would be that so little was said because there was in fact so little to say in this regard that would have served the church's growing faith in him as Messiah.[6] Or to put it another way: Jesus' early years were unexceptional. They flowed along within the banks of the ordinary—a conclusion that would give added plausibility to the astonishment of both family and neighbors at the turn of events that led to his public career.

But having acknowledged the paucity of our information, it is equally important that we take note of the facts we do have and begin to assess them carefully. Even the skeletal data outlined above may bring us closer to a better understanding of Jesus' early years and his experience of his father in particular.

For example, that he was the first-born in this family of four younger brothers and several sisters is obviously not without significance.[7] In most cultures, expectations and hopes center on the eldest son as on no other, but this was true to a special degree in the world of Jesus.[8] As a consequence it is reasonable to imagine he would have been made to feel an especially heavy weight of responsibility to and for his parents. In Jesus' famous parable of "the prodigal son" (Luke 15:11-32), it is the elder son who stays home and takes care of the farm, the younger one who leaves to "sow wild oats." Is this an accident?[9]

And what are we to think of the name given to this first-born? It is true that in that day "Yeshua" was as common as John is in ours, but neither then nor now was the naming of a child a triviality, and especially not then. "Yeshua" means "Yahweh is saviour (or helper)" and brings to mind one of the great "savior figures" in Israelite history—the Old Testament Joshua.[10] This name also bears witness to the piety that must have characterized his home, as do the names of his parents (Joseph and Miriam) and those of his brothers—Joses (an abbreviation of Joseph), James (Jacob), Judah, and Simon. All come from the earliest and most important periods of biblical history (the brothers, like the father, all bearing the names of biblical patriarchs). Obviously this was a family rooted and grounded in Jewish faith, a fact attested to as well by what the early church historian Eusebius reports concerning Jesus' brother James, who after Jesus' death became the leader of the Jerusalem church (Gal. 1:19; Acts 15:4-29). He was "holy from his birth," Eusebius tells us in a quote from Hegesippus.

> He drank no wine or intoxicating liquor and ate no animal food; no razor came near his head; he did not smear himself with oil, and took no baths. He alone [Hegesippus continues] was permitted to enter the Holy Place, for his garments were not wool but of linen. He used to enter the Sanctuary alone, and was often found on his knees beseeching forgiveness for the people, so that his knees grew hard like a camel's from his continually bending them in worship of God.[11]

Clearly the family of such a son must have been a deeply religious one.

The same cannot be said, however, of the place where this family lived, Nazareth of Galilee. Concerning the village itself there was a proverb: "Can anything good come out of Nazareth?" (John 1:46), and only four miles to the northwest was Sepphoris, the seat of government for the Roman occupation prior to the building of Tiberias in 18 C.E.[12] Galilee as a whole, with its some two hundred cities and villages, was heavily populated and seethed with conflicting movements and traditions. Here as nowhere else in Palestine pockets of orthodox Judaism lived side by side with pagan ways typical of the wider eastern Mediterranean world of that time.[13] Small wonder that this was the region where revolutionary movements originated that were eventually to bring disaster to the Palestinian Jews. Jesus did not then grow up in a simple, happy world, even if the home he lived in was undoubtedly anchored in Jewish piety.

As an artisan in wood, his father's vocation would have been visible and attractive to the young Jesus, and there is no reason to doubt that he followed in his father's footsteps. Whether this meant he became a village carpenter, as traditionally thought, or was more like a contractor, as Buchanan has argued (building on a larger scale and supervising a work force),[14] his trade in either case required competencies of no mean proportions. Indeed, writes David Flusser, carpenters were regarded as particularly learned people in Jesus' day and as such were often consulted when a difficult problem was under discussion. This is no proof that either he or his father was learned, Flusser adds, but "it counts against the common idyllic notion of Jesus as a naive and amiable, simple manual workman."[15]

His marital status is puzzling. The assumption has been that he was celibate, since no wife is mentioned in the canonical records. But celibacy poses certain problems in the Judaic tradition. In the Babylonian Talmud (Kiddushin 29a) we read that a Jewish father had five principal responsibilities to his son: to circumcise him, redeem him, teach him Torah, teach him a trade, and find him a wife. Kiddushin 30a reports that "Raba said to R. Nathan b. Ammi: Whilst your hand is yet upon your son's neck, [marry him], viz., between sixteen and twenty-two. Others state, between eighteen and twenty-four." If these traditions were already in vogue in Jesus' time (and there is no reason to think otherwise), why then did Jesus' father not find him a wife? An answer is difficult to come by, especially in the light of the very strong emphasis on being married in that culture. With this information in mind, William Phipps has argued that we should look at the possibility that he *was* married after all.[16]

But there is another possibility which Phipps fails to consider that might have had a bearing on all this. As may be inferred from the total silence regarding Jesus' father in the Gospel accounts where his family is mentioned (Mark 3:31-35; 6:1-3), it is likely that Joseph had died prior to the time of Jesus' mission at thirty.[17] When might this death have occurred? If it is true that Jesus' father failed to find him a wife, perhaps he died quite early, before Jesus was old enough for a wife to be found for him. On the other hand, Joseph's death could not have happened when Jesus was still a small child, for there were four younger brothers and several sisters in this family.[18] This would suggest a date for this traumatic event sometime during Jesus' early teenage years. In that case, as eldest son (in accordance with the traditions of his culture), the mantle of leadership in this family would have fallen on him. That the people of his village reportedly referred to him on the occasion of his visit there at thirty as "son of Mary" (Mark 6:3) instead of "son of Joseph," as one might have expected, may reflect these circumstances.[19] It appears, Connick states, that due to these circumstances (Joseph's death) "Mary's first-born son became the breadwinner and family head at an early age."[20] Given these conditions it is not difficult to imagine why his marriage was delayed.

So we are not completely in the dark about Jesus' early years. There are indeed many fruitful hints and suggestions, even in the few facts we do have. Unfortunately there is much that remains obscure, and we cannot go very far on this basis alone before imagination threatens to embellish the tradition in questionable ways.

Supplementary Data

There is another way of proceeding, however. It is one that has become the "stock in trade," so to speak, of psychoanalysts and psychotherapists generally, although its application to the records of Jesus' life, so far as I know, has only rarely been attempted. Instead of working forward from the sparse records of childhood into adulthood, psychohistorians frequently work backward to childhood from analogous experiences in the life of the adult. This would mean that data relevant to the theme "Jesus and his father" is not confined to factual reports out of his childhood, but can be derived as well from statements and experiences of the adult Jesus in which "fatherhood" or "fathering" is a factor. This approach anticipates that every one of us has a reservoir of "father-type" experiences from which we draw and which contributes, negatively or positively, to every new experience we have in this regard.

What then can be said of Jesus' experience of "father" as it comes to expression in the events and teachings of his adult life? It is well known that almost everything he reportedly said or did is relevant to this question, so pervasive is this theme in the Gospels. Our task at this point is to identify those texts in which the emotional dimensions of this facet of Jesus' teaching are most tangible. I suggest that these are evident at four points especially: (1) in Jesus' unique use of "Abba" (father) as a way of invoking God; (2) in what he taught about the importance of father-child relations; (3) in the portraits of "fathers" in his parables; and finally (4) in explicit references to fathers in several of his more memorable sayings. I will discuss each of these topics briefly and conclude with a developmental hypothesis.

(1) That Jesus conversed with God in a way that differed from that of

his contemporaries is one of the more assured and significant results of modern Jesus studies.[21] And the difference illuminates graphically the theme "Jesus and his father." A comparison of the prayers of Jesus with those of his peers in Judaism reveals that Jesus, like no other Jew we know of in that time, frequently (perhaps regularly) addressed God as "Abba."[22] "Abba" is the Aramaic diminutive of "Ab" (meaning father) and was the typical way a small child of that time would address a trusted and beloved father (although adults too might address other warmly regarded superiors in this manner as well).

"Father," of course, occurs in many religions as a designation of God, and especially so in the scriptures of Judaism (Deut. 32:6; Ps. 89:26; Mal. 2:10).[23] Nowhere, however, in the extant literature before or contemporary with Jesus do we encounter another example of prayer in which God is directly invoked as "Abba." The reason is not hard to fathom. Used as an invocation, this word out of daily life would have been regarded as too intimate, too familiar, lacking in respect (the more traditional terms of address were "Lord" or "King").[24] "The complete novelty and uniqueness of *'Abba* as an address to God in the prayers of Jesus," writes Jeremias, "shows that it expresses the heart of Jesus' relation to God."[25] It is not surprising, therefore, that the reality to which the name Abba pointed (God's fatherly love) permeates his teaching. "Call no man your father on earth," he once said to his disciples, "for you have one Father who is in heaven" (Matt. 23:9). The meaning of this striking admonition is not, obviously, that Jesus objected to small children calling their own fathers Abba, but that his disciples should refrain from addressing honored teachers or other distinguished figures in that manner. For Jesus "Abba" was a sacred word reserved only, among adults, for God. It was, Jeremias suggests, his most important linguistic innovation.[26]

What might have been the antecedents in Jesus' life of such an extraordinarily intimate, confident and childlike way of speaking to God? One thinks immediately of the baptismal experience at the Jordan. Jeremias believes that the "sonship" that broke in upon Jesus there had revelatory importance for him, and that "Abba" was his response.[27] But even so, this experience would represent only its "near" background. There are, no doubt, emotional "echoes" here as well of events still further back. "Abba" is first and foremost a child's word. Its primal home is the deep affectional bond fashioned between father and son early in life. As

Jesus himself once said, "No one knows a son except a father, and no one knows a father except a son" (Matt. 11:27//Luke 10:22).[28] Surely, then, Jesus' love of the word *Abba* as a term for addressing God not only reflects his experience at the time of his baptism, but must hark back as well to his earliest experiences with his personal father in his family of origin.

(2) But before pursuing this line of thought further, it is important that we turn to a second group of texts in which a very similar orientation comes to light: Jesus' sayings about children. The Gospels record two episodes in particular that picture Jesus relating to children, and in both instances he is said to have singled this relationship out as a supremely important one.

The first such occasion is described in Mark 9:33-37 (Luke 9:46-48//Matt. 18:1-5). The disciples had been arguing over which of them was "the greatest." In response Jesus took a small boy, "put him in the midst of them" and "taking him in his arms," he said, "Whoever receives one such child in my name receives me; and whoever receives me, receives not me but him who sent me." Especially striking in this instance is Jesus' act of taking this boy into his arms (omitted by Matthew and Luke). It was a warm paternal gesture that dramatized the word he is reported to have said on this occasion.[29] The issue at hand was male hubris (who will be greatest). True greatness, Jesus implies, is not to be found where men usually seek it but in their receptivity to children. "Whoever *receives* one such child receives me. . . ." Few Gospel stories are as revelatory as this one of Jesus' heightened paternal feelings during this stage of his life.

In the second scene in which children play a role, it is others who take the initiative in bringing children to Jesus "that he might touch them" (Mark 10:13//Luke 18:15) and "lay his hands on them and pray" (Matt. 19:13). The disciples try to prevent their approach, but Jesus is indignant at their attitude (according to Mark), declaring that "to such belongs the kingdom of God" (Matt. 19:14//Mark 10:14//Luke 18:16). Then we are told that he made this startling pronouncement: "Truly, I say to you, whoever does not receive the kingdom of God like a child shall not enter it" (Mark 10:15//Luke 18:17). In Matthew this saying is attached to the previously discussed incident and phrased in a slightly different way: "Truly, I say to you, unless you turn and become (or "become again") like children, you will never enter the kingdom of heaven" (Matt. 18:3).[30] Here it is the child and not the reception of the child that is focused on. But in what sense? Matthew's account intimates that it was the child's "humility" that Jesus had in mind. "Whoever *humbles* himself like this child, he is the greatest in the kingdom of heaven" (Matt. 18:4). But more than that may be at stake. "'Become a child again,'" writes Jeremias, "means: to learn to say *'Abba* again."[31] It is not only humility, then, but the whole trusting, relaxed, and uninhibited rapport of children with their fathers that seems to have been especially appealing to Jesus. It is again only Mark who reports that upon saying this, Jesus "took the children in his arms . . ." (Mark 10:15).

(3) What Jesus felt about "fathers" and the "father-son" relationship is also reflected in his parables. While only two of them speak explicitly of fathers and sons (Luke 15:11-32; Matt. 21:28-31), a strong, fatherly-type man is a recurrent figure in the forty or so stories he told.[32] A few examples would be the father who was already in bed with his children when a "friend" came knocking on his door at midnight wanting bread (Luke 11:5-8); the farmer who confidently sows, then "sleeps and rises" while the seed grows, "he knows not how" (Mark 4:26-29); another farmer who tries to calm his anxious servants in the face of a dangerous overgrowth of weeds among the wheat (Matt. 13:24-30); the optimistic sower (Mark 4:3-8); the concerned shepherd who goes looking for the lost sheep "until he finds it" (Luke 10:29-37); the superforgiving king (Matt. 18:23-35); the firm, yet polite "father Abraham" (Luke 16:19-31); the risk-taking merchant who was displeased when one of the men to whom he had lent money did nothing with it but protect it (Matt. 25:14-30//Luke 19:12-27); the fair but generous vineyard owner (Matt. 20:1-16); the wonderfully caring Samaritan (Luke 10:29-37); and of course that unforgettably gracious father in the story of the prodigal son and his upright elder brother (Luke 15:11-32). Several of the men who play the leading role in these parables are not of especially good character (the wicked judge, Luke 18:1-8; the dishonest steward, Luke 16:1-8a), but even they are portrayed in a remarkably friendly, humorous light. But the dominant figures in the great majority of Jesus' stories are fatherly types in positions of responsibility who are shown executing those responsibilities in forceful, competent, but often surprisingly gracious ways.[33]

For Jesus, obviously, father figures of this type were attractive. They function quite often, in fact, as his spokesmen (Matt. 13:29-30; 18:32-33; 20:13-15; 25:26-27; Luke 15:31-32; 16:25-31). He was not unaware of the dynamics they create. To a father's request (in one of his parables) that his sons go to work in the vineyard, one of them curtly replied, "I will not!" but later repented and went, while his brother said politely, "I go, sir!" but then did not go (Matt. 21:28-30). It is well known how Jesus expanded on this theme in his famous parable of the prodigal son (Luke 15:11-32). Long before Freud, Jesus took note of ambivalence toward fathers as a disturbing factor in human relations, but it seems his own attitudes in this respect were unusually positive.

(4) Finally, several additional sayings of Jesus should be noted where fathers are explicitly referred to and instruction given regarding them. One such is the citation of the command to honor father and mother in the reply given to a certain young man who had asked him what he should do to inherit eternal life (Mark 10:19//Luke 18:20//Matt. 19:19). How important to Jesus respect for parents actually was is also revealed in his sharply worded critique of *qorban*, a practice among the rabbinic elite whereby a son could avoid financial obligations to his "father or mother" by dedicating the support that he owed them to the temple (Mark 7:9-13).[34] However, he too taught that "father and mother and wife and children and brothers and sisters, yes, and even his own life," must be "hated," were this to prevent someone from being "my disciple" (Luke 14:26//Matt. 10:37f.). The most sharply formulated saying of this type was one spoken to a potential follower who wished first to bury his "father" (Luke 9:59//Matt. 8:21), to whom Jesus said: "Leave the dead to bury their own dead" (Luke 9:60//Matt. 8:22). At issue, perhaps, was his treasured new-found experience of *God* as gracious father, devotion to whose will (as this was unfolding through his mission) takes priority over everything else. A moving testimony to the depth of his faith in this regard is his beautifully off-hand statement about the greater goodness of God as father compared to the flawed goodness of human fathers. "What man of you [what father], if his son asks him for bread, will give him a stone? Or if he asks for a fish will give him a serpent? If you [fathers] then, who are evil, know how to give good gifts to your children, *how much more* will your father who is in heaven give good things to those who ask him!" (Matt. 7:9-11//Luke 11:11-13).

Could Jesus have spoken of fathers and the father-child relationship so often and in such utterly realistic yet positive terms, had he not had a deeply meaningful experience somewhere along the way with his own personal father? To me the answer seems obviously, "No!" but other researchers have judged differently, and a brief look at a few of their observations may help focus some of the issues at stake here, and how the data just surveyed might best begin to be assessed from a psychological point of view.

Questionable Hypotheses

The Jungian psychiatrist Edward Edinger, in his book *Ego and Archetype*, states his opinion that Jesus was probably an illegitimate child who "demonstrates some characteristic features of the individual who has no personal father."[35] When the personal father is missing, more particularly, when he is completely unknown, as may happen with an illegitimate child, there is no layer of personal experience to mediate between the ego and the numinous image of the archetypal father. This, Edinger says, produces a kind of hole in the psyche "through which emerge the powerful archetypal contents of the collective unconscious."

> Such a condition is a serious danger. It threatens inundation of the ego by the dynamic forces of the unconscious, causing disorientation and loss of relation to external reality. If, however, the ego can survive this danger, the hole in the psyche becomes a window providing insights into the depths of being.[36]

This colorful characterization is useful in that it starts us thinking about the historical antecedents of a key feature of Jesus' emotionality. But what evidence is there, one might ask, that Jesus was illegitimate, or that he had a "hole in his psyche" or suffered in the manner described? The issue of illegitimacy does arise in the setting of the "infancy narratives" in Matthew and Luke, where we are told of Mary's premarital pregnancy (Matt. 1:18) and of Joseph's initial reactions and his decision "to divorce her quietly" so as not "to put her to shame" (Matt. 1:19)—but not once elsewhere in the entire body of New Testament literature (Gospels, Acts, Letters) are these events (Mary's virginal pregnancy *or* Joseph's reaction) ever again noted or referred to, much less discussed, a fact difficult to explain were these traditions known or deemed important.[37] What *is* known and reported (and seemingly taken for granted) is that Jesus was "born of a woman" (Gal. 4:4) whose husband was Joseph (Matt. 1:16) and that Joseph was the father of Jesus (Luke 4:22; John 1:45; 6:42).[38]

But even were it true that Jesus' father was someone else (perhaps someone unknown to him), would there necessarily be a paternal "hole in his psyche" making him vulnerable, as Edinger puts it (in Jungian terms), to the threatening archetypal contents of the collective unconscious? Does not virtually every child, even one whose biological father is missing or unknown, have father surrogates of some sort to relate to and with whom various "father"-type experiences are internalized and combined? Whatever therefore might be concluded about Jesus' parental circumstances, we can, I think, be sure of this: in growing up he encountered and had to deal with a "father" of one kind or another. That Jesus had no history of an earthly father to draw upon in working through or experiencing his relation to God as father is, in my opinion, clearly out of the question.[39]

For this and other reasons I am more drawn to portraits of Jesus and his father in which at least *something* is hypothesized regarding what Jesus' earlier relationship to his father (or father surrogate) might have been like. Foremost among these are the sketches of those who since Freud have examined the Gospel accounts of Jesus' life from the point of view of developmental psychoanalysis. As the review of studies of this kind in the Appendix indicates, however, even among this group opinions and judgments vary considerably. For example, what most impressed religious psychologist R. S. Lee as he approached the Gospels from this point of view was that Jesus "showed no signs of mother-fixation, but appears to have completely resolved his Oedipus Complex, not merely as a child, but in his sublimist relations with God the Father."[40] In other words, for Lee Jesus is an ideal figure who must have been remarkably successful in resolving the typical childhood conflicts of a son with his personal father to have arrived as an adult at such a relaxed and confident faith in God as Father.[41]

The opinions of a New York psychiatrist, Matthew Besdine, who also examined the life of Jesus from this perspective, vary considerably from Lee's conclusions in this regard.[42] In Besdine's view, far from being a model of emotional and spiritual health, Jesus shows signs of belonging to a gallery of neurotic geniuses (Goethe, da Vinci, Michelangelo,

Proust, Dostoevsky, Freud) whose developmental backgrounds almost invariably turn out to include a distant or strained relation with their personal fathers and a much too intense and prolonged bond with a certain "Jocasta-type" mother (Jocasta being the excessively involved mother of Oedipus). Indeed, he writes, "it could be argued that the life of the historical Nazarene, as we know it from the Gospels, bears the clear imprint of Jocasta-mothered genius." As evidence Besdine cites

> the ineffectual, older father; the astonishing intellectual precocity; the final rejection of the mother; the absence of any sexual relations with women, yet the intense sympathy for the prostitute; the vanity, the egocentricity and fig-blasting temper; the exclusively male band of disciples and companions; . . . the search for an all-loving all wise and powerful Father; the guilt, the atonement, the courting of and achievement of personal destruction, and finally, the staggering accomplishment.[43]

This too is a provocative portrait, but again, questions arise. What, for example, is the evidence that Jesus' father was "older"? Our sources tell us nothing about his age. Also, as Besdine himself notes, "Jocasta-mothered geniuses" are notoriously ambivalent and ill at ease in their attitudes toward fathers. So, if Jesus were a person of this type, with an "ineffectual father" and an excessively close-binding mother, how are we to account for the fact that the tie to the mother was seemingly sundered at the time of his mission, and that subsequently he was as relaxed and positive about fathers (and about God as father) as he seems to have been? Indeed, the impression we have from our sources is not that Jesus was *seeking* an all-wise and all-loving spiritual father at that time, as Besdine puts it, but that he had found one.

On the basis of the evidence assembled thus far, I must therefore agree with Lee to this extent at least—that Jesus as a child apparently had made a fundamentally successful passage through the important emotional transactions of the oedipal years, and at thirty (during the time of his mission) exemplified a remarkably positive and insightful appreciation and love for "fathers" both personal and divine.

An Alternative Hypothesis

Nevertheless, Besdine's portrait is not completely off the mark. For one thing, the experience Jesus is said to have had at the time of his baptism (when "the Spirit" came upon him and a "voice" affirmed him as a "beloved son") must apparently have met some prior need in his life for it to have become the turning point in his career that it seems to have been. In other words, Jesus' experience at his baptism of being graciously affirmed as "a son" pleasing in God's sight appears to have answered to a prior deficiency or problem in that very regard. This observation might be thought to contradict what has just been emphasized about Jesus' paternal emotions. The contradiction is only apparent, however, and compels me at this juncture to make an important clarification in my reconstruction of his psychological development.

True as it would appear to be that a strong affectional bond existed between Jesus and his personal father, there are, nevertheless, reasons for believing this relationship was sorely tested, plunging him into an ordeal of more than ordinary emotional stress and strain. One biographical datum especially lends support to this hypothesis and goes a long way, I believe, toward explaining many unique features of Jesus' adult life and mission: namely, his father's premature death. This proposal will be fleshed out in subsequent chapters, but it may be noted here that such an event is bound to have had an emotional impact on Jesus, especially if it occurred (as I conjecture) in early adolescence before a wife had been found for him.

Jesus' baptism would indeed then have been a "turning point," a "restorative" experience, a new beginning, a "second birth," as intimated in chapter 3, but not because he had had no earlier "birth" into the kind of emotional freedom a father can help a child attain. Rather, between his initial experience of "father" and his second (at the time of his baptism), something had been lost, or nearly so. My conclusions at this point are similar to those of a famous literary critic, J. Middleton Murry, whose reflections on the life of Jesus are dated but perceptive nevertheless:[44]

> Jesus' childhood was of the utmost significance to him. He thought of it, in later years, as an age of completeness, and he felt that his life as a little boy had been fuller and truer than his life as a man,

> and that in growing up he had lost something infinitely precious that it was worth the whole world to regain. For that something he found many names; sometimes he called it the Kingdom of God, sometimes Life itself. It was a condition of security, of spontaneity, of freedom from all doubt and division. He never forgot it.

As this passage implies, there was not only a "light" side but a "dark" side to Jesus' experience of the "father." "In growing up he lost something infinitely precious." Is there any further evidence of this loss? I believe there is, first of all in what the Gospels intimate regarding Jesus' relationship to his mother.

5

Jesus and His Mother

He has much to say of a father's love for his children, but nothing of a mother's love. It is true that the father in question is God, but even the "prodigal son" is not welcomed by his mother. We must conclude, therefore, that his father's memory was more precious to him than his living mother, who did not understand him and whom he turned away when she and his brothers came to take possession of him.[1]

"What have you to do with me?"

The behavior of Jesus toward his mother during his public mission is an enigma frequently noted but seldom probed. The result has been that a pious haze often obscures the most obvious features (in this regard) of the picture of him in our oldest sources.[2] The enigma, of course, has to do with the tensions that seem to have characterized this relationship. In our inquiry thus far I have implied that Jesus' estrangement from his family involved the entire family, but we have also become conscious of the fact that this family at this time of Jesus' life was incomplete. Jesus' father is missing in the Gospel accounts of Jesus' mission at thirty, and the most likely reason is that he had died some years earlier. If there were tensions, then, between the thirty-year-old Jesus and his family, these did not center on his father but on his mother and siblings. She (and they), not the father, are the ones who thought him "beside himself" and went to Capernaum to "seize him" (Mark 3:21, 31-35). She (and they) are the ones whom he refused to see on that occasion, and who prompted the sharp rejoinder: "Who are my mother and my brothers? Here are my mother and my brothers! Whoever does the will of God is my brother, and sister, and mother" (Mark 3:33-35).

Further evidence of these tensions, especially as they relate to the mother, is not hard to come by. Virtually everything our sources tell us about her and her eldest son in this period of their lives suggest that their relationship at this time was strained. Not only would he not see her when she and his siblings came to Capernaum seeking him, but later on when a certain woman blessed his mother in his hearing, his response was to refocus the blessing on "those who hear the word of God and keep it" (Luke 11:27f.). The portrait of this relationship in John's Gospel reinforces the impression created by these scenes. There, in two incidents (the wedding at Cana, John 2:1-11; and his words from the cross, John 19:25-27),[3] Jesus is said to have addressed his mother in the same somewhat formal manner he is reported to have used with women generally (Matt. 15:28; Luke 13:12; John 4:21; 8:10; 20:13). He does not call her "mother," but "woman" (John 2:4; 19:26). While the term is not impolite, it is certainly unusual and conveys a certain detachment and lack of closeness. "What is peculiar," summarizes Raymond Brown, "is the use of 'Woman' alone (without an accompanying title or qualifying adjective) by a *son* in addressing his *mother*—there is no precedent for this in Hebrew nor, to the best of our knowledge, in Greek."[4]

Consistent with this is the substance of what John's Gospel reports transpired between mother and son on the occasions referred to. In the story of the wedding at Cana, Jesus' mother is shown turning to him for help in a domestic crisis. The wine had run out, and she wanted him to do something about it. His response was curt: "What have you to do with me, woman?" (literally: "what to me and to you, woman?"; John 2:4).[5] On the cross, in his final words, he displayed filial concern when he transferred responsibility for his mother from himself to a beloved disciple: "Woman, behold your son . . . Son, behold your mother" (John 19:27). But here again he did not address her as his "mother." Both scenes convey the impression of a Jesus who is prepared and wanting to do his duty by his mother, but who does this in a detached, unemotional way.

This impression is reinforced by what Jesus says, or rather does not say, in his teachings about mothers generally. If we turn once again to his parables to see if there might not be some intimations there of his feelings toward mothers, what is notable, first of all, is how few of the stories he told mention women at all. In fact, a quick survey will reveal only four instances: the widow in the parable of the unjust judge (Luke 18:1-8); the woman baking bread in the parable of the leaven (Matt. 13:33//Luke 13:20f.); the ten maidens waiting for the bridegroom (Matt. 25:1-12); and the woman who finds a lost coin (Luke 15:8-10). These parables stand in contrast to some thirty parables in which men are the dominant figures. And what is even more astonishing is that in none of these stories in which women appear are they portrayed as mothers with children. In short, there is nothing here that would even remotely compare with Jesus' parabolic portraits of fathers and sons.

Turning to Jesus' sayings, the gap is even more striking. Apart from the generalized references to honoring "father and mother" and to his true mother, brothers, and sisters being those who do God's will, mothers are mentioned only once, and this in a passing reference to the tragedy of women with suckling babies in the catastrophic days he foresaw would be coming (Mark 13:17//Matt. 24:19//Luke 21:23; 23:29).

Is this remarkable silence about women generally, and mothers in particular, accidental? I find it difficult to think so, especially in the light of several instances in which the silence seems almost tangible. A notable example would be Jesus' famous story of the departure and homecoming of the prodigal son. Why, in this longest of Jesus' parables, is the focus so exclusively on the father? Is there no mother in this home, and does she not also rejoice at her lost son's return? This rather puzzling omission recurs in Jesus' story about a man who knocked on his friend's door at midnight hoping to borrow three loaves of bread (Luke 11:5-8). Why in this instance does the friend reply from within: "Do not bother me; the door is now shut, and my children are with me in bed . . . ?" Does this man have no wife with him in bed? Do these children have no mother?[6]

The impression grows that the tensions between Jesus and his mother were not only real but long-standing. They not only flared up in tense episodic encounters with the mother herself but left their imprint on his teachings. Why was this so? Where did these tensions originate, and why by this time in his life had they not been resolved?

The Gospels themselves hint at the answer in their silence regarding Jesus' father. It was his death, I will now argue, and the role that Jesus thereafter had to play in this family, that is the key to unlocking the enigma of Jesus' puzzling attitudes toward mothers. Before saying more about this, however, it will be necessary to digress briefly and recall what modern psychology has had to say about mother-son relations generally. This research provides the background against which I will then elaborate a developmental profile that will engage us, in one way or another, for the remainder of this study.

Mothers and Sons

Modern psychologists are unanimous in emphasizing the fundamental importance of the initial bond between mother and son for the son's future emotional well-being. It is the mother who (by virtue of the symbiotic bond created through pregnancy, birth, and nursing) typically functions as the child's primary caretaker in the first months of life. As such, she is also the foremost agent in establishing that all-important sense of trust or confidence in life without which a child can scarcely survive at all. Regarding this relationship the religious psychologist Antoine Vergote has written:

> She who bears the new life and places it in the world is also she who surrounds it with her care and her warmth, who nourishes it, and who always remains, on the level of symbolic representation, the figure of unconditional acceptance. From the total acceptance by the mother, the child derives affective security. The experience and the memory of maternal availability normally confirm the child in its personal value and develop in him a fundamental confidence in life and in humanity, which is a necessary condition for the acquisition and maintenance of the sense of personal identity.[7]

With each new stage of childhood, however, the role of the mother becomes more complex, for already in her child's second year she must begin to balance her embracing receptivity and love with the recognition of her child's need for autonomy and a growing relation with the father.[8] And this shift of emotional focus from mother to father becomes even more important in the case of a son during the first sexual awakening of the oedipal stage from about three to six (which typically centers on the mother), if he is to bring closure to what will otherwise become an inhibiting and constricting incestuous relationship and acquire a firm sense of masculine identity. Thus, the mother has the demanding task of first birthing, nurturing, and loving her son in the first months and years of his life, but then gradually "letting go" in order to foster his autonomy and relation to the father, so that he can experience an increasingly meaningful paternal rapport and eventually leave his parental home to establish one of his own.[9]

It is the complexity of this process that gives to the oedipal years of childhood their uniquely dynamic and sometimes traumatic role in human maturation. For a mother to love her child so deeply and then to let him go is emotionally wrenching. No less so is it for a son to be loved in this way and then to relinquish his intimate relationship with the mother for that more autonomous, more demanding relationship with the father. Few sons grow to manhood having completed the emotional transformation required of them at this point, and some, because of significant unresolved problems, enter adulthood inwardly divided, ambivalent, and "neurotic."[10]

Does this developmental sketch provide us with any further clues as to what may have been happening between Jesus and his mother when he was "about thirty"?

The Hypothesis Revisited

It must be admitted, first of all, that in some respects what has just been written about mothers and sons generally only deepens the mystery of Jesus' attitudes toward mothers. For if it is true that it is the mother who is primarily responsible for engendering in her son confidence and "trust," and if, in addition, she must foster his freedom by releasing him for an increasingly important relationship with the father, then it would have to be said that Jesus' mother appears to have played her role well in Jesus' early years. In any case, there is ample evidence for asserting that one of the outstanding characteristics of the *adult* Jesus was the evocative power of his faith (trust) and an equally remarkable capacity for uninhibited, autonomous action.[11] Furthermore, there is no reason to doubt that Jesus made an essentially normal emotional transition from his mother to his father during the crucial oedipal years. There would seem to be, therefore, no reason to trace the source of Jesus' tensions with his mother back to any maladaptive dynamic in their relationship in his earliest formative years.

Where, then, shall we look for their origins? We must return again at this point to the developmental scenario that I have already indicated might well hold the key to this enigma. After an essentially normal, happy childhood, Jesus' father died, leaving him heir to his father's role in the family left behind. This traumatic event might well have been the primal impetus in the unfolding of many of the most unique and outstanding traits of the adult Jesus, including his peculiarly strained relations with his mother.

To visualize more concretely how and why Joseph's death could have had such consequences, however, it will be necessary to undertake a fairly difficult exercise in historical imagination. It is important, first of all, that we try to identify as specifically as possible what some of the major social and emotional consequences of such a death might have been for an elder son.

(1) To begin with, it is important to recall what bearing such a death might have had on the sheer economic survival of this family. If Jesus, before this death, was indeed working with his father in carpentry, as the Gospels intimate, it will now fall to his lot to shoulder this trade by himself, for he will now have become his family's chief means of support.

(2) In addition to financial responsibility, the emotional, social, and spiritual leadership once vested in his father will now gravitate toward him as well. The sense of obligation will mount to assume virtually all of the impossible burdens of surrogate husband and father in a family in which he is really still a son.

(3) From this circumstance, an extremely difficult inner conflict will ensue over which is to have priority, and for how long: his father's family or his own; his father's wife or his own; his father's children or his own. With each passing year (and the postponement of his marriage), this conflict will become increasingly acute.[12]

(4) At the same time, the demands of heading such a large family at such an early age will prove to be a stimulus to the development of latent talents. Jesus will have to learn quickly how to care for and manage in an efficient, competent manner. Studies of the impact of parental loss on children have amply documented this aspect of such a trauma. Many an outstanding leader, they have shown, has become that way through translating the struggle for mastery, following the death of a parent, into an accelerated personal development leading to superiority in a given field.[13] Here, in part at least, may lie the origins of that magisterial sure-

ness and wisdom that radiate so strongly from the Gospel accounts of Jesus' mission.

(5) On the other hand, this same demanding role may also pose certain psychological risks, certain "temptations." To become suddenly "father" in a world in which it would still be normal to be "son" sets the stage for a reawakening of oedipal ambivalence, even where the emotional hazards of that stage of life have been satisfactorily surmounted. Children deprived of their fathers at adolescence are prone to a heavy sense of responsibility, bordering at times on grandiosity, especially if they are *first-born* sons.[14]

(6) As time goes on, the relation to the mother may prove to be increasingly problematical, as she, on her part, tries to cope with the loss of her husband by leaning more and more on this resourceful eldest son, thereby intensifying sibling rivalries.

(7) A welter of emotions may accompany these developments: anger at the premature loss of his father, guilt at taking his place, fear of going too far or not far enough in this complex role, idealization of the lost father, anxiety over unknown catastrophes yet to come.[15]

The list of possibilities could be extended, but already this much may serve to shed light on the tensions between Jesus and his mother at the beginning of his fourth decade. An adolescent son, even an emotionally healthy one, who suddenly finds himself thrust into a surrogate husband-father role will understandably experience an identity crisis. And such a crisis, it must now be emphasized, can only be resolved by an act that can brook no compromise. A clear and definite choice will have to be made between mother and "God." The network of pseudo-obligations in which his life to this point has been enmeshed will have to be broken. And when the break comes, it is understandable if the mother is mystified and might even think her son "beside himself" (Mark 3:19b-21). Counselors know only too well the blindness of mothers toward the deepest needs and necessities of the sons on whom they are dependent for emotional and physical support.

A personal dilemma of this nature might have been resolved by the son leaving home, marrying, and founding a home of his own. I have personally known several "elder sons" whose fathers died in adolescence, who did precisely that, at about the same age as Jesus when he left Nazareth.[16] Instead of marriage, however, it was the prophetic preaching of John the Baptist that summoned Jesus out and away from his maternal home into the wider world. And with the help of modern psychological research we can begin to sense why.

The quandary in which Jesus found himself due to the loss of his father must have been an increasingly severe one. By his thirtieth year, he must have been groping (unconsciously perhaps) for a next step, a way out of the ultimately sterile, guilt-producing surrogate role in which he found himself.[17] John the Baptist's warning of impending catastrophe, his call to repentance, his promise of forgiveness, his baptism, as well as the awesome paternal figure of John himself were the catalysts that moved him at last to take action. And it is clear now why the words "from heaven" immediately after the baptism, "You are my beloved son, with you I am well pleased," reached him at the depths. Jesus had found God and his father again. Simultaneously he found himself as well. The claim of his mother upon him had been broken by renewed contact with his "Father in heaven" (Matt. 11:25-27//Luke 10:21f.).[18]

But what, more precisely, would this sonship mean? The answer was born, I suggest, in what additionally Jesus is said to have experienced in the immediate aftermath of his baptism.

6

Satan

Jews were familiar with the belief that evil spirits of a minor character sometimes appeared to human beings and sought to mislead them, or even gained access into them, assuming control of their personalities and deranging their minds, either temporarily or permanently. But there is no example in Jewish literature before the time of Jesus in which Satan appears to a man face to face and engages him in conversation.[1]

Jesus' Consciousness of Satan

The Synoptic traditions inform us that following his baptism Jesus was driven by the Spirit into the wilderness and there tempted by Satan (Matt. 4:1-11//Mark 1:12-13//Luke 4:1-13). By this they suggest that, far from resolving the tensions that may have warred within him at this time, his experience at the Jordan in some sense activated them and brought him to a personal crisis. It was not in spite of his baptism that Jesus subsequently isolated himself in a forty-day ordeal of fasting and prayer, but because of it. Satanic temptations were the consequence of the gracious revelation of the "father" that broke in upon Jesus at the Jordan.

Strange as it might seem, there is a compelling psychological logic to this portrayal of Jesus' baptism and its aftermath. It is a recurrent experience in counseling that as a client approaches a critical point in therapy, emotions that once orbited around parental figures are reactivated and "transferred" to the counselor. For a brief moment, in fact, the counselor becomes the client's mother or father.[2] This transference in turn facilitates a return (or regression) to earlier phases of his life where the emotional problems that trouble him may have originated. In the safety of the therapeutic relationship, he may then reexperience them in both their positive and negative aspects and consciously work them through, as an adult, in new, more satisfactory ways.[3]

If my suggestion is correct that Jesus at his baptism (with John the Baptist's help) found his "father" again, then it is only to be expected that such an experience would have awakened not only earlier positive feelings toward his father but traumatic aspects of that relation as well. That such there were is intimated by the likelihood that Jesus' father had died, perhaps during his early teens, leaving him as eldest son in charge of his father's widow and a relatively large family of four brothers and several sisters. The so-called "temptations" of Jesus, I will now try to indicate, may reflect a critical stage in Jesus' coming to terms with the perverse emotional and ideational consequences of this tragic event.

But before pursuing this possibility further, it will be necessary to pause briefly and ask whether it is legitimate to approach these temptation narratives in this manner (especially the Q accounts, Matt. 4:1-11//Luke 4:1-13). To begin with, are we allowed to rely on them for insight into the inner world of the *historical* Jesus? Or are they instead a product of the early church, as many scholars now seem to think? The issues in this instance are admittedly complex.[4] But there is a major unsolved problem confronting those who question the historicity of these narratives as to who, if not Jesus, their author or authors might have been. After all, the entire early church was convinced that Jesus was the resurrected Messiah and as such now lived in a realm far above satanic principalities and powers (1 Cor. 15:24; Col. 2:15; Eph. 1:20-21). Who, then, in that church would have dared to imagine that at some point in his earthly life Jesus was actually *tempted* by Satan—to fall down and worship him—if there were not a historical basis for doing so?[5] It might be added that in Jewish thought as well it was inconceivable that the *Messiah* would be tempted in this manner. Rather, it was anticipated that when the Messiah came, Satan would be dethroned, not gradually but by a single mighty act of power.[6] The notion, therefore, that Satan might enter into a conversation with the Messiah with the intent of leading him astray was almost unthinkable.[7]

At the same time, what was apparently foreign to the thinking of first-century Jews and unlikely as a construction of early Christian imagination is hinted at again and again in sayings of Jesus that are generally accorded the highest degree of historical authenticity. It is widely acknowledged, for example, that the Jesus of history was unique in envisioning the realm of evil as cohering under a single satanic power, and especially so in viewing this power as tottering on the brink of defeat.[8] It was this vision that gave him boldness in exorcism (Luke 11:20//Matt. 12:28//Luke 13:16), in prayer (Luke 22:31f.), and in rebuke ("Get behind me, Satan" Mark 8:33). "I saw Satan fall like lightning from heaven," he once exclaimed (Luke 10:18). But if such was the case—and this at the very onset of Jesus' public mission—it follows that already before that mission something must have happened to have given Jesus this unprecedented conviction.

This conclusion is not simply conjectural. In a pivotal parable Jesus defended his success in exorcism by referring to a "strong man guarding his castle" who was defeated by one still "stronger than he" (Luke 11:21f.). It is generally acknowledged that Jesus is here referring to *himself*. He is the "stronger" one, who in face-to-face combat defeated the "strong man" (Satan) and thereby set in motion those events that would eventually lead to his defeat! This parable in particular, it would seem, points to just such a contest with Satan as the temptation narratives describe.

Thus, the evidence favoring a point of origin for these accounts in a personal experience of the historical Jesus (one which he would have shared at some point with his disciples) is considerable—sufficient, in any case, in my opinion, to justify our studying them with this possibility in mind. If in doing so they turn out to be thematically and psychologically compatible with what is otherwise known about Jesus, then this evidence too, perhaps, may be added to the arguments favoring their historicity.[9]

Temptations

If the temptation narratives are historical, what then are we to make of these accounts? What is it that Jesus actually experienced on this occasion? A cluster of early twentieth-century psychiatrists, in their assessments of Jesus' "mental health," were quite sure that here, if anywhere, we encounter certain unmistakably malignant "symptoms."[10] Thus, they said, when Jesus speaks of "Satan" approaching him and taking him to the pinnacle of the temple (Matt. 4:5/Luke 4:9), or the top of a mountain that overlooks the world (Matt. 4:8/Luke 4:5), or when he fantasizes about turning stones into bread (Matt. 4:3/Luke 4:3), he is only too obviously hallucinating. And that can only mean that on this occasion, at least, he must have crossed that thin line that separates sanity from insanity, normalcy from psychosis.

At the opposite extreme in the reading of these stories are those who view them as "symbolism" pure and simple. In his baptism, so the traditional interpretation goes, Jesus became conscious of a messianic vocation. But then he was left to ponder how he would go about exercising this momentous responsibility. After considering and rejecting three possibilities, he clothed his conclusions in the colorful manner in which we now have them. The form of the narrative is thus a kind of "artistry" which should not be confused with its substance.[11]

This symbolic reading above all, it seems to me, needs to be challenged if we are to grasp these accounts aright. There is a lesson to be learned at this point from recent developments in the study of Jesus' parables. An older tradition of parables-study searched for the hidden "truth" that was thought to be embedded in these evocative stories. But more recent investigation has begun to ask whether the parables are not themselves the "truth." Instead of thinking of Jesus arriving at certain ideas which he then tried to "illustrate," perhaps his imagination was just this pictorial and metaphorical in the first place. The parables are not simply pedagogical devices; they are the stuff and substance of his thought-world.[12]

If that was the case with the parables, then we might do well to consider that it was equally true with respect to the temptation narratives. Satan was precisely this real to Jesus, the visionary experiences just this surrealistic, and the testings just this auditory and dialogical. These narratives are not simply window dressing but a compact summary of how Jesus experienced, met, and overcame that force which threatened him at the core of his personal existence.[13] If not "hallucinations," then at least emotional issues of considerable severity are alluded to here. What are they?

Two of the temptations begin, "If you are the son of God" (literally: "if a son, you are, of God "). Already in our analysis of Jesus' baptism the point was made that "son of God" does not necessarily imply a messianic consciousness ("if you are the Messiah"), since "son of God" was not commonly regarded as a messianic title in the time of Jesus. Rather the "sonship" alluded to here might well have been personal, existential, or prophetic, corresponding, in some sense, to the divine intimacy exhibited by the first-century B.C.E. miracle worker, Honi the Circle-Drawer. What Jesus was struggling with in these temptations was not how he, as Messiah, was going to carry out this role, but an ecstatic consciousness of intimacy and rapport with God ("thou art my son . . .") that left him vulnerable and susceptible to inflated, grandiose ideas.

The temptations themselves may be classified in a twofold way. In two of them Satan solicits courses of action that might appear, at first glance, to be logical consequences of the newly experienced rapport with God. "If you are a son of God [if you are in such intimate rapport with God], command these stones to become bread. . . . If you are a son of God, throw yourself down [from the pinnacle of the Temple]. . . ." A third temptation, however, seems to bypass the issue of sonship and invites Jesus rather to forsake his relation to God altogether and become Lord of the universe by worshiping Satan instead. "All these I will give you if you will fall down and worship me." So the issues posed are not only what kind of son to be, but whether to be a son of God at all. Why not rather be a son of Satan and rule the world?

In all instances, however, the actual content of these temptations is similar. All three seek to entice Jesus into fantasizing extraordinary feats of the most grandiose nature (turn stones into bread, fall safely from a great height, rule the world). But what in substance is Satan actually confronting Jesus with in these seemingly bizarre suggestions? It is difficult not to see in the background here *messianic* fantasies of one sort or another, for to work mighty signs and to rule the world were the then prevailing expectations of what a miracle-working Messiah would do when he appeared. If that were so, then Jesus would be telling us in these temptation accounts that in the aftermath of his baptism he was sorely tempted by Satan to think of himself as the long-awaited Messiah who by signs and wonders would one day deliver his people and rule the world.[14] At the same time, however—and this, of course, would be the main point—he decisively rejected these solicitations as a satanic ploy tantamount to idolatry with the help of words of Scripture that came to mind at crucial moments of this ordeal: "Man shall not live by bread alone . . . You shall not tempt the Lord your God . . . You shall worship the Lord your God and him only. . . ." These citations are all from the opening chapters of Deuteronomy (8:3; 6:13; 6:16), an obviously important section of Scripture for Jesus, as can also be gathered from his references to the Shema (Deut. 6:5) in Mark 12:29f., and the decalogue (Deut. 5:16-20) in Mark 10:19.[15]

In summary then, it is not, as traditionally thought, the Messiah who is here being tempted, but Jesus, fresh from an experience of repentance, forgiveness, and "sonship," who is being tempted by messianism. In the account of his temptations, Jesus relates how, after having encountered God at his baptism, he was assailed by thoughts of messianic grandeur but decisively rejected them.

Parallels

But what shall we make of this experience psychologically, and how relate it to our developing profile of Jesus' inner world? From what has already been said, it would appear, first of all, that the Satan of these narratives, like God, is also something of a father-figure, albeit a very negative one.[16] This is most obviously the case in the final temptation (following Matthew's order), in which Satan openly invites Jesus to worship *him* in place of God. In this instance he is clearly, in Jesus' eyes, the embodiment of patricidal ambition. He seeks to entice Jesus to usurp the role of his true Father (God) and rule the world in his stead.

That a satanic reality should play a role of this kind in psychic life may, at first glance, seem strange. A look at a few "case histories" in which something similar is at work might therefore be helpful. By examining analogous cases, we can become better acquainted with the various meanings "Satan" has had in human experience generally and hence what he might have signified for Jesus uniquely.

It is well known, for example, how a demonic figure was also a disturbing force in the life of the Protestant reformer Martin Luther. Erik Erikson, in his psychohistorical study of Luther (*Young Man Luther*), notes that "even a few days before his death Luther saw the devil sitting on a rainpipe outside his window exposing his behind to him. Such 'reality' always existed for him along side Aristotle and St. Augustine, St. Paul and the Scriptures."[17] Just these few comments alert us to the "anal" disposition of Luther's devil. Likewise, Luther, in flaunting him, resorted to farting, defecating, cursing, throwing, and "holy sarcasm."[18] Erikson concludes that all this was an escape valve for Luther, necessary because of a still active residue of "defiance" in Luther's personal make-up. Luther's devil then, as Erikson describes him, was a kind of negative parent surrogate upon whom (along with the Pope) he vented that stormy early childhood rebellion against his father, which remained to the end of his life such a disturbing feature of his personality.[19]

Freud has also given us a very provocative study of a young man beset by the devil in his study of "A Neurosis of Demoniacal Possession" in the experience of Christopher Haitzmann, a seventeenth-century painter.[20] In his case too, as Freud describes it, the devil was something of a father surrogate, and a rather pathetic one. He first approached Christopher in the aftermath of his father's death, at a time in his life when he was troubled by his inability to find employment. His initial disguise, so to speak, was that of an "honest old burgher with a flowing brown beard." Strangely, however, the devil's profferings of "wizardie and black magic . . . money and amusements" were all rejected by Haitzmann. What finally won him to the devil's side was his offer to help "in every way and give him aid" in overcoming the state of melancholy into which he had fallen. The nine-year pact thereby concluded read as follows: "I give my bonde and pledge myself unto this Satan for to be unto him even as a soone of his bodie and after 9 yearses to belong unto him bodie and saule."[21] The story does not end there, but this much will already indicate that Haitzmann's devil is quite different from Luther's. Freud wrote that "a man who has fallen into a melancholie on account of his father's death must have loved that father deeply."[22] Thus, Satan in this instance is not an "enemy" to be flaunted, as in Luther's case, but an almost motherly figure (he actually had maternal breasts in some appearances) to whom Haitzmann looked for comfort in the midst of his rather excessive dependency needs.

Returning to the temptations of Jesus, it is evident, to begin with, that neither of the cases reviewed could be said to be exactly parallel. In fact, they differ considerably from each other, suggesting that Satan, or the devil, wears many masks. In one instance he is the provoker of "anal defiance," and in another he solicits an excessive dependency once provided by a now deceased father.

Grandiosity

What was Satan, then, for Jesus? I have already alluded to the implicit grandiosity of Jesus' satanic temptations. In each instance, Satan confronts him with the possibility of acting in superhuman ways, of achieving spectacular power over nature, over people, and finally over the world, by ruling in God's stead. Dare we imagine that Jesus was actually tempted by bizarre thoughts such as these?

The temptation narratives, of course, clearly intimate as much, and were it so, it might be possible to imagine why—if, in any case, we once again recall that Jesus may have lost his father in early adolescence. I have already noted in chapter 6 that one of the traumata that such a son may suffer is that of becoming suddenly powerful and hyperresponsible in a world in which only a short time before he was dependent and responsible to another. Before his father's death Jesus was his father's eldest son. His father was the one in charge. Now everyone turns to him for leadership and help. Now, suddenly, even though still a son, he is compelled to act like a father himself in his father's own household. This psychologically dangerous situation prefigures, on a human scale, the temptations of Satan on a cosmic one. In those temptations Jesus' newfound identity as son of God (his spiritual "father") was made vulnerable to the "impossible possibility" of ruling God's world in his stead. Understandably, a "son" in such circumstances will find himself contending with fantasies of greatness, fantasies that he knows, in his more sober moments, to be totally illusory. If it so happens that he lives in a time when visions of the coming of a miracle-working Messiah are rampant, these may well determine the more precise form that such fantasies might take.

Thus neither Luther's devil (the evoker of anal defiance) nor Haitzmann's (an object of overdependence) was the Satan of Jesus. Yet he too was tempted and "driven" by the Spirit into the wilderness, there to wrestle with psychic forces that must have tormented him earlier. Now, however, the issue had come to a head. Now—in the wake of that utterly compelling experience of sonship at his baptism—he would have to decide, once and for all, which of the conflicting identities that warred within him was really his. Is he his father's beloved son (the child he once was prior to his father's death)? Or is he that grandiose figure that rose up to haunt him at the promptings of "Satan" (the hyperresponsible and controlling person he was tempted to become in the wake of his father's death)? At the crucial moment he was able to say "No!" "Begone, Satan!" (Matt. 4:10). The experience of a humbler, more authentic sonship was now too strong within him to be taken captive by such an inflated image of himself.

Later on he would ask his disciples what it profits a man to gain the whole world and lose (or forfeit) his soul (Mark 8:36//Matt. 16:26//Luke 9:25), and teach that to find your life you first had to be willing to lose it (Mark 8:35)—that no spectacular sign would be given to authenticate who he was (Mark 8:11-12); that those who want to rule over others are mistaken and should seek rather to be servants (Mark 10:43f.); that only those who become like children can enter the kingdom of God (Mark 10:15); that "everyone who exalts himself will be humbled, but whoever humbles himself will be exalted" (Luke 14:11). Sayings such as these (and others), so obviously related in some manner to his own personal ordeal, would be remembered as among the most characteristic words of his historic career.[23]

Theological Postscript

It only needs to be emphasized how deeply Jesus must have felt about the victory he had won in divesting himself of these satanic delusions. If the temptation ordeal just looked at was the occasion alluded to in the parable of the defeat of the strong man (Luke 11:21f.)—and we know of no other—then, in saying no to grandiosity of this kind, Jesus believed he had reached a turning point of far-reaching significance for himself and the world.

Christian theology might do well to consider whether in this judgment he was not precisely right. The temptation narratives (and this would be added reason against their having been formulated by the later church) portray the conquest of Satan by Jesus as having happened before his resurrection, before his death on the cross—even before his public mission. Salvation dawned, this would suggest, when Jesus, in humble, loving obedience to his "heavenly Father," rejected those fantasies of messianic grandeur set before him by Satan and determined to do only what God willed for his life. Viewed developmentally, such a step is crucial in a son's maturation; and in Jesus' case too, it seems, this was the psychic victory that at last enabled him to offer the world his creative contribution.[24]

Before we go on to indicate what that contribution was, however, and how what we have been discussing thus far might bear upon it, there is an additional facet of Jesus' psyche at thirty that bears closer scrutiny: his sexuality.

7

Sexuality

Spricht so ein Mann, für den Ehelosigkeit ein Ideal wäre? [Would a man for whom celibacy was an ideal speak in this manner?][1]

Alternatives

As a way of gauging the accuracy of the picture of Jesus' inner world that has been emerging in our study thus far, there are few more important topics for consideration than the nature of his sexual outlook. The opening of this previously taboo subject in modern times is by no means simply a consequence of our penchant for discussing intimate matters publicly. It is much more the result of our growing awareness of the importance of sexual attitudes as indices of emotional maturity.

Being fully human, Jesus too must have been sexual in one way or another. But how? Three somewhat contradictory answers have been put forward in recent studies: (1) he was celibate, as traditionally assumed, but this was because he was homosexually oriented; (2) on the contrary, the assumption that he was celibate is mistaken—he may, in fact, have been married; (3) although celibate, he related to women in ways that were exceptionally open, accepting, and intimate, given the mores and traditions of his culture.

As a way of approaching this sensitive and difficult topic, I will review and critique each of these suggestions. A more adequate understanding of Jesus' sexuality emerges, I will argue, when the data referred to by the proponents of these views is seen in the light of the developmental profile of Jesus emerging in our study thus far.

Homosexual?

The most prestigious recent exponent of the possibility that Jesus might have been homosexually oriented is Canon H. W. Montefiore, Vicar of Great St. Mary's Cambridge, who made this suggestion in a much-discussed speech to the conference of Modern Churchmen at Somerville College Oxford, in the summer of 1967.[2] Something of the public furor that followed is echoed in J. A. T. Robinson's *The Human Face of God*, which defends Montefiore's proposal as at least as worthy of consideration as the more traditional idea that Jesus was without sexual feelings altogether.[3]

Montefiore's treatment of this subject is , however, not very substantial. It is based primarily on inferences drawn from a rather limited list of reasons why men generally do not marry. Either they cannot afford to, he says, or there are no girls available, neither of which would apply to Jesus. "Vocational celibacy," he adds, "is also no explanation as to why Jesus remained celibate during the thirty years prior to his baptism by John, for it was only at that time that his messianic vocation first became clear to him." Montefiore concludes that there is thus only one reason remaining for Jesus' failure to marry: homosexuality. And in a single sentence, he gives what he apparently considers to be the conclusive supporting evidence: "According to the Gospels, women were his friends but it is men whom he is said to have loved."[4]

A more elaborate argument in support of this hypothesis can be found in Noel I. Garde, *Jonathan to Gide: The Homosexual in History*.[5] There, among three hundred biographies of noteworthy figures from the past three thousand years (all of whom, he claims, "have been referred to in responsible printed works as being homosexual . . ."), is a relatively lengthy sketch of Jesus' life from this point of view. Garde begins by singling out Matthew 19:12 (the "eunuch" saying) as evidence that sexual activity was "particularly loathsome and unattractive" to Jesus. "To be really holy, a man should castrate himself."[6] Jesus was, however, at first unaware of the true reason for the antisexual feelings that welled up within him. Among the Jews in that day, says Garde, homosexuality was so obnoxious that it would never have entered Jesus' mind that his feelings against sex with women might mean not that he was sexless but that he had sexual emotions of another kind.

Only after he began recruiting disciples did he first become aware of the possibility of "love for a man," and especially through his fondness for the "beloved disciple" John. Even then, Garde speculates, Jesus found it difficult to comprehend what was happening, so "repressed" was this side of his experience. But there must have come a moment when the reality of what he felt became unmistakably evident. The shock was so great that Jesus panicked.

> The reckless actions of Jesus at the temple, predictably certain to bring a fatal arrest and end to his career, would be comparable to those of the more familiar young homosexual of Puritan moral character who, upon discovering his homosexuality, is so horrified and disgusted that he joins an army and throws himself into the most dangerous actions with the hope of getting himself killed and thereby putting an end to his insoluble problem.[7]

In assessing these proposals, Montefiore's suggestion that the data available hardly permits of any other explanation of Jesus' celibacy than homosexuality should be noted first of all. Surely people fail to marry for reasons other than those he mentions. Furthermore, there is also little or no evidence for the contention of both Montefiore and Garde that Jesus preferred friendships with men rather than women. That "Jesus' most intimate associates were members of his own sex," Tom Horner summarizes, is only "what we would expect at that time and in that place."[8] In fact, what seems unusual in this particular cultural context is not his affection for men but the degree to which women also were involved in his mission.

But the really weighty objections to viewing Jesus as homosexually oriented, in my opinion, come at two other points: his insightful teachings about marriage and his exuberantly positive representations of "fathers" and God as father.

Regarding Jesus' teachings about marriage, Montifiore and Garde say nothing except to call attention to his word about "eunuchs" (Matt. 19:12), which Garde believes is evidence that heterosexuality was "loathsome and unattractive" to Jesus. In reality, this saying assumes that heterosexual relations are normal, while observing that there are reasons, nevertheless, why some abstain ("there are eunuchs who have been so from birth, and there are eunuchs who have been made eunuchs by men, and there are eunuchs who have made themselves eunuchs for the sake of the kingdom of heaven").[9] Of course, had we no other statement from Jesus than this one, Garde's point might still carry some weight, but Jesus' heterosexual attitudes are made quite explicit in his famous defense of fidelity in marriage, which begins by referring to the way God created human beings male and female and then (on the basis of Genesis 2:24) declares that it is "for this reason a man shall leave his father and mother and be joined to his wife, and the two shall become one [flesh]" (Matt. 19:5//Mark 10:7). It is difficult to imagine how Jesus could have been more forthright, for his reference here to "one flesh" is a quite explicit statement regarding the sexual bond and the encompassing unity it brings about between married couples.[10] Marriage, as Jesus viewed it, is consummated through the union of bodies in sexual love. And that is why he emphasized that what God (in this manner) "has joined together," should not be "put asunder" (Matt. 19:6//Mark 10:8).

A comparison of these words with those of Leonardo da Vinci, whose latent homosexual orientation is well documented, is instructive. He once wrote that

> the act of procreation and everything that has any relation to it is so disgusting that human beings would soon die out if it were not a traditional custom, and if there were no pretty faces and sensuous dispositions.[11]

How different are the thoughts of Jesus! In his view, sexual relations between a man and woman in marriage, far from being "disgusting," are an aspect of the created order through which God himself acts to unite husband and wife ("what God has joined together . . .").[12]

But just as important (perhaps more so) for assessing the proposal that Jesus might have been homosexually oriented is the previously noted regard he shows for "fathers" and fathering, and his corresponding attitude toward "mothers." To explain adequately why these matters are relevant requires a more extensive review of the psychogenesis of male homosexuality than would be appropriate at this point in our discussion. Perhaps it will suffice to note that numerous studies have demonstrated that a significant contributing factor in many instances of male homosexuality appears to be a parental milieu characterized by a dominating, possessive, sexually prudish mother and a weak, absent, or aloof father.[13] Where this is the case, obviously, it will be difficult for a son to form the positive "father identification" that is so vital to his securing a firm masculine identity and autonomy from the mother. "The father's libidinal and aggressive availability," writes Charles Socarides, "is a major requirement for the development of gender identity in his children, but for almost all prehomosexual children the father is unavailable as a love object for the child."[14] According to Fisher and Greenberg there does not appear to be a single even moderately well-controlled study of parental attitudes among male homosexuals that shows that they refer to their fathers positively or affectionately. On the contrary, they write:

> With only a few exceptions, the male homosexual declares that father has been a negative influence in his life. He refers to him with such adjectives as cold, unfriendly, punishing, brutal, distant, detached. . . . He easily fills the unusually intense, competitive, Oedipal role Freud ascribed to him.[15]

A specific and especially germane case in point is André Gide's reinterpretation of Jesus' famous story of the prodigal son.[16] As Gide, a well-known author and outspoken homosexual, retells it, the prodigal son did not return to his father in a repentant mood, nor did he confess his unworthiness and receive forgiveness. Rather, after a lengthy argument with him over why he had left home in the first place (in which he defeated his father), he turned to his mother. She is the real reason for his returning, he tells her.

"When I am with you," he says, "I scarcely understand how I could ever have left the house."

"You will leave it again?" the mother asks.

"I cannot leave it again," he replies, admitting later on that in saying so he has resigned himself to a life of failure.

The conversation with the mother closes with a request that she kiss him on the forehead as she used to do when he was a little boy.[17]

Gide, in short, has refashioned Jesus' story of a son's reconciliation with his father (and a father's love for his wayward son) into a tale of a son who is still paternally alienated and hostile returning home to his mother after a failed attempt at living apart from her.

By contrast, as we have seen, Jesus at thirty appears to have become a free man so far as his mother was concerned, and during his public mission he emerged as a passionate advocate of paternal reconciliation, especially reverence toward God as father. "Father," he taught his disciples to pray, "hallowed be thy name . . ." (Luke 11:2).

Married?

Far more in harmony, then, with what we know of the psychology of Jesus is the suggestion that he might have been married—a possibility that has been ably argued by William Phipps (among others) in a book-length study provocatively entitled *Was Jesus Married?*[18] Phipps cites the following evidence in support of his thesis: (1) it was almost inconceivable in that time and place for a Jewish young man *not* to marry, for the Jewish community thought marriage to be a religious duty mandated by Scripture (Gen. 1:28);[19] (2) Jesus often talks like a married man, especially when he speaks of marriage itself and how wrong it is for husbands to divorce their wives; (3) the intimacy that seems to have existed between Jesus and Mary Magdalene points to a relationship of a very special kind. In fact, Phipps contends that she might well have been the wife in question. However, sometime prior to his public mission, he speculates, Mary left him for a life of sin in Magdala, a fishing village of ill repute by the Sea of Galilee. There Jesus found her again, cleansed her of her demons, and won her back as both wife and disciple. Indeed, Phipps argues that it is this traumatic event that might well lie in the background of Jesus' unusually firm stand against divorce, for it was through this experience, he conjectures, that Jesus came to understand the redemptive power of marital fidelity.

Phipps is to be commended for having brought this possibility to our attention and for having argued it so intelligently. This challenge to consider that Jesus might have been married is definitely a step forward in the discussion of his sexuality. It strains the imagination, however, to think that this actually was the case, when not a single tradition to this effect has survived either in the canonical literature or virtually anywhere else.[20] It is true, of course, that there is something unusual about the scenes in the Gospels where Jesus' relations with women are portrayed (see below). But there is not the slightest evidence that he was husband to any one of them. The best hypothesis is still that Jesus never married.[21]

Nevertheless, Phipps and others are certainly justified in pressing the question as to how, if Jesus did not marry, this fact can be squared with the overwhelming emphasis on marriage among Jesus' contemporaries (not to speak of his own positive outlook toward marriage in his teachings). If Jesus did not marry, then surely some reason must be given as to why he chose not to do so. I have already called attention to the likelihood that this issue may be wrongly put. Responsibility for marriage in his culture rested not with the son but with his father. The father, not the son, was the one the community held accountable for finding a wife and arranging the wedding. The question then is not why Jesus chose not to marry, but why his father failed him in this regard. Phipps also entertains this question but then too quickly assumes that if Joseph fulfilled his other traditional responsibilities toward Jesus—dedicating him, circumcising him (as the infancy narratives imply that he did), teaching him Torah and a trade—then he must have found him a wife as well.[22] But this assumption overlooks the possibility discussed earlier that his father might have died (during Jesus' earlier adolescence, perhaps) *before* the time had arrived when he could have done so.[23] In that case, Jesus (as eldest son) would have then had to assume the role of leader of his deceased father's rather large family (Mark 6:3)—a circumstance that might well have led to a delay in his founding a family of his own. I suggest, then, that neither homosexuality nor paternal neglect were the most likely background factors in Jesus' celibacy, but that his failure to marry was a consequence of circumstances resulting from his father's premature death.

My conclusion from all this is that Jesus very likely would have married were it not for the pressures and responsibilities that came into play in his parental family in the wake of his father's death. As the time approached when he might have broken free of these and founded a home of his own, however, another calling intervened—the summons at his baptism to be a prophet to God's people Israel in what he came to believe was a crucial hour of reckoning.[24]

Women

It is in this role as prophet that we see him during his public mission and in this context that we read those scenes in the Gospels which portray Jesus actually relating to women—scenes like the one in which a "woman of the city" wets his feet with her tears and dries them with her hair (Luke 7:36-50); or another in which an unnamed woman pours expensive ointment over his head (Mark 14:3-9//Matt. 26:6-13; cf. John 12:1-8);[25] or the episode involving a certain Mary, who was commended for her impulsive neglect of household duties in order that she might listen to his teachings (Luke 10:38-42); or the witty repartee with a Syrophoenician widow (Matt. 15:22-28); or his telling defense of a woman taken in adultery (John 8:3-11). I refer also to the comments in Luke and Mark that women accompanied and ministered to him, some of whom had previously been healed by him "of evil spirits and infirmities" (Luke 8:2//Mark 15:40f.); and to the fact too that women (and only women) were with him at the end during his crucifixion (Mark 15:40//John 19:25//Matt. 27:55//Luke 23:49). What are we to make of these encounters with women?[26] On this basis, what more, if anything, can be said about Jesus' sexual outlook and attitudes?

It is evident, first of all, that even though men made up the inner circle of his disciple group (Mark 6:6b-13), women "thronged" to him too[27]—especially, it would appear, women who were alienated and in need. "Tax collectors and harlots go into the kingdom of God before you" (Matt. 21:31), was Jesus' own summing up of what he saw happening in the repentance movement that swirled around John the Baptist and himself. It is apparent too that in responding to these throngs Jesus did not make the sharp distinctions between men and women drawn by the religious and cultural leaders of his time. Even at the risk of creating suspicions, he was apparently as receptive and pastoral in his relations to a repentant "*woman* of the city" who was a "sinner" (Luke 7:37) as he was to an equally sinful *man* of the city (Luke 19:1-10); as willing to enter into conversations with a troubled Syrophoenician *widow* (Matt. 15:22-28) as with a troubled Roman centurion (Luke 7:1-10); as eager and ready to share his ideas with friends who were women (Luke 10:38-42) as with friends who were men. The impression one gets is that what counted in his eyes was "neither male nor female" (Gal. 3:28) but the person and his or her need. Schalom Ben-Chorin writes that he knows of nothing in rabbinic literature to compare to the kindness of Jesus' words to repentant prostitutes.[28]

It does not necessarily follow, however, that Jesus was consciously intent on bringing about equality among men and women, as some have portrayed him.[29] Nor is there much of a basis in our sources for determining to what extent his relationship with any of the women whose names are mentioned was unique or special to him, although there can be no doubt that a friendship existed between him and the two unmarried sisters Mary and Martha.[30] Obviously, Jesus touched the emotions of many women through his genial caring approach, and some of them loved him dearly for it (Luke 7:36-50; Mark 14:3-9; Matt. 26:6-13; John 12:1-8). That he was romantically attracted to any of them is another question. Mary Magdalene's prominence in the Gospel traditions is attributed to the dramatic nature of her healing (Luke 8:2) and the important role she played in the emergence of resurrection faith (Matt. 27:56, 61; Mark 15:40, 47; 16:1; Luke 24:10).[31]

If there is any additional point to be made as to the emotional or motivational dynamic at work in these relationships, it might be to call attention to the *fatherly* qualities that appear from time to time in Jesus' relationships with women. In our study so far I have been stressing Jesus' self-identity as "son," but it must now be emphasized that being a son is the decisive step, developmentally, in becoming like the father. Jesus at "about thirty" was also very much in process of becoming a father-figure in his own right. Whatever feelings women might have had for him, he would appear to have related to them as "daughters," and explicitly addresses them as such on several occasions (Mark 5:34, 41/Luke 13:16). In Mark 5:41, in fact, the tradition has preserved his Aramaic *ipsissima vox*, "*talitha cumi*" ("little lamb, arise")—a hint, perhaps, as to how highly prized the memory of his tender, fatherly manner of speaking was among the early Christians.[32]

In yet further explanation of this fatherly facet of Jesus' personality, it may be appropriate, perhaps, to refer once again to the hypothesis that during some part of his adult life he was a surrogate father to his younger sisters (Mark 6:3) in the family of their deceased father. His stance toward women during his public ministry was thus shaped in part, I suggest, by his role as head of his father's family. In any case, at this time in his life his sexual feelings seem to have retreated behind the role of "father" and become visible, if at all, at two points only: in the saying about the danger of committing adultery in one's heart (Matt. 5:28), and in his observations regarding eunuchs (Matt. 19:10-12). Whatever else might be made of these sayings, it must at least be emphasized that the man who spoke them was heterosexually self-aware and candid. He knew what it was like to "look at a woman lustfully," and he was fully conscious of the difference between a eunuch who is such from birth or mutilation, and one who is celibate because of inner choices and discipline "for the sake of the kingdom of heaven" (Matt. 19:12). Vermes suggests that a plausible background for this saying might be first-century C.E. Jewish opinion regarding the life of continence appropriate to one called to be a prophet.[33] If Jesus lived what he taught, then these sayings could be taken as reflections both of what he personally experienced and of how he sought to cope with his own sexual feelings during the time of his public mission. Although he found women attractive, he did not look at them lustfully but kept this side of his emotions in check for the sake of that larger mission that engaged him in this specific period of his life.[34]

Wider Implications

It might be added as some further indication of the long-range significance of the issue under discussion in this chapter, that it is doubtful if Christianity would be much affected by the discovery that Jesus had, in fact, married.[35] Married or celibate, his was a marriage-oriented, heterosexual, monogamous posture. On the other hand, it is difficult to imagine that Christianity would be the same religion had he actually been homosexual. The naivete at this point of otherwise sophisticated theologians is perplexing, especially when they try to assure us that a homosexual Jesus would leave untouched the church's historic faith in him as "perfected" man.[36] Between mother-oriented personalities and cultures and father-oriented personalities and cultures a gulf opens up that is decisive for the shape of human and religious experience. "It is precisely because homosexuality alarms the father-identifier," writes Gordon Taylor, "that the Jews found it a particularly objectionable feature of the worship of Baal. Equally, only because it offers a solution to the mother-identifier could it become a regular feature of the worship of mother deities."[37]

> If we are right in assuming that mythologies provide us with important clues to unconscious preoccupations, then we must certainly attend to the powerful and popular myth associated in Greece with the name of Dionysos, which has many parallels throughout the Mediterranean world. In this myth, the central figure is a young man, the son of a mother goddess. He fertilizes his mother and is subsequently killed or castrated. Generally he then descends into hell or the underworld, whence he is rescued by his mother, only for the cycle to be repeated. . . . The myth that ultimately replaced that of Dionysos and his homologues was that of a young man [Jesus], a son, whose preoccupation was with his father.[38]

However, in order for this "young man," this "son" (as Taylor speaks of him) to become the world-transforming figure he has been and is, a challenge had to be faced, a calling embraced, a mission undertaken. The "revelation" Jesus received at his baptism and the inner clarity and strength won through his battle with Satan had to be shared with others.

8

Generativity

It is not necessary to speculate about Jesus' psychology. We know *that he was moved to act and speak by a profound experience of compassion. And we* know *that the Abba-experience was an experience of God as compassionate Father.*[1]

Identity and Generativity

Up to this point our study has been focused for the most part on topics and themes in which the emotional side of Jesus' life is most clearly visible (family, conversion, father, mother, Satan, sexuality). As a consequence, we have paid very little attention so far to its wider social, moral, and religious dimensions. There are, of course, obvious reasons for this. It is the very nature of a psychohistorical inquiry to be predisposed to what can be known about the *inner* dynamics of the figure being studied. An investigation of this kind that did not relate the insights about inner dynamics to the more obvious features of a given individual's historic achievement would, however, certainly be open to criticism. Jesus was, after all, more than a devoted son "preoccupied with his father" (as the quote from Taylor at the conclusion of the previous chapter describes him). In or around the thirtieth year of his life, he accomplished something extraordinary in the moral and religious realm that has had an ever-widening impact on the world ever since.

Achievements of this kind cannot, of course, be ultimately explained, but they can be better understood. Several observations have already been made as possibly useful in fostering such an understanding. A high-intensity "mothering factor," for example, is clearly in the background of men of genius generally, and it is possible that this might have been the case with Jesus as well.[2] "Parental loss" has also been identified in recent research as a catalyst in the achievements of an extraordinary number of "eminent" individuals. The potential genius, Eisenstadt has argued, translates the struggle for mastery following the death of a parent into a personal development that leads to a high degree of competency.[3] That something of this nature may have been in the background of Jesus' achievement at thirty has also become evident in the course of our inquiry.

It must be borne in mind, however, that Jesus' "genius" and the achievements that flowed from it were of a very specific kind. At the beginning of the fourth decade of his life (Luke 3:23), soon after his baptism and temptations, the Gospels tell us, he became a prophet-evangelist with an intense concern for the welfare of a certain group of people: "the lost sheep of the house of Israel," as they are referred to in Matthew 10:6 and 15:24.[4] It was at this time, in the midst of this specific evangelistic mission, that he "came into his own," so to speak. What is needed, then, is some more encompassing psychological perspective that might contribute to our understanding of Jesus' *vocational* achievement as an evangelist among the disaffiliated and how this particular accomplishment might relate to what we have learned about him thus far.

Does such a "more encompassing psychological perspective" exist? I believe it does, and suggest that we turn for help in this regard to the research of Erik Erikson and Daniel Levinson on life-stage developments during early adulthood and the "Age Thirty Transition" (Levinson).[5] Without denying Freud's insight that we are heirs as adults to the repercussions of the emotional transitions and crises of our childhood (those of the oral, anal, and oedipal stages especially), Erikson insists that these by no means exhaust what can be said about human emotional development. Adulthood too, he writes, is marked by acute transitional crises and biologically anchored, phase-specific challenges. During the so-called "latency" of late childhood, for example, certain competencies are (or are not) attained, and at puberty (at a point when our bodies are reaching the apex of their physical maturity) the strengths gained through life's earlier stages need to be integrated (with the help of some budding sense of vocation, usually) into a unique self-identity ("this is me"). Soon thereafter, Erikson notes, there is typically the desire for "intimacy" and marriage, and then having children and caring for them. In other words, it is during this period in life that a man begins to "find himself" vocationally. He then moves out of his parental home into the intimacy of marriage and a home of his own, has children, and becomes a parent himself.

Transitions of this kind, successfully negotiated, give rise to certain intrinsic strengths or "virtues" (as Erikson refers to them). Those emerging from a successful transition through puberty into marriage, according to Erikson, are characterized by "fidelity" (being true to oneself and others) and "love" (the capacity for affection and intimacy). Having children stimulates a cluster of qualities having to do with "caring," "caring for," and "taking care of" the coming generation.

For this latter child-caring phase—in some respects the apex of the life cycle, in that the well-being of the whole is so radically dependent upon it—Erikson has coined the term "generativity." Men who successfully enter and pass through it, he writes, are not simply "productive" or "creative" in an individualistic sense, but link themselves to others (their wives first of all) in "taking care of" that which their creativity has produced (their own children, to begin with).

As with all life stages, however, this one too can be disrupted or retarded and then belatedly accelerated by factors other than the normal ones. And once released, "generative care," notes Erikson, may encompass a far wider circle than that of the immediate biological family. Anyone who by whatever means gains a clarified sense of himself and his role in the world may experience (as a natural outgrowth of this development) a desire to unite with others on behalf of others, and a surge of caring. As such, generativity is the polar opposite of that stagnant, self-indulgent narcissism that may progressively consume the lives of those who miss the way at this critical juncture in life.

Erikson's insights have been supplemented by the research of Daniel Levinson who, on the basis of in-depth interviews with a cross section of forty American men, succeeded in pinpointing the more precise nature and age-period of several of the adult stages Erikson had only roughly outlined. Especially germane to a study of Jesus is Levinson's discovery that the acute turbulence in many men's lives during their late twenties and early thirties is not an abnormality, as sometimes thought (a symptom of delayed adolescence, for example), but a recurrent, altogether typical experience resulting from crosscultural factors inherent to the complex task of becoming an adult. As evidence of the transcultural nature of the stages he identifies (and their rootedness "in the nature of man as a biological, psychological and social organism"), Levinson cites a number of texts from a variety of cultures outlining adult transitions roughly as he has done.[6] In the talmudic "Sayings of the Fathers," for example, the stages of life from age five to one hundred are identified, and thirty is mentioned as the time in life when "full strength" is attained (*Avoth* 5, 24).

More specifically, he found, the men he had interviewed had entered adulthood in two rather distinct stages: a first more casual, experimental mode (during their early twenties) when there was as yet little awareness of the limits or brevity of life; and a more urgent, serious mode (during their later twenties and early thirties) when the realization was born that life is short and if anything significant or authentic is going to be accomplished, a start will have to be made *soon*, or it will be too late.[7] As a result, between twenty-eight and thirty-three a sometimes traumatic "Age Thirty Transition" ensued during which a given individual's accomplishments to this point were tested against a still latent, unrealized "Dream" and found to be wanting. This Dream, Levinson reports, had "the quality of a vision, an imagined possibility that generates excitement and vitality."[8]At the beginning of the Age Thirty Transition it was often still poorly articulated or encased in grandiose aspirations only tenuously connected to reality (as in the myth of the hero). But now, it was felt, the hour had struck when this Dream had to be defined and lived out quite concretely. Otherwise it would die, and with it an essential sense of "aliveness and purpose."[9]

Surprisingly, the men he interviewed often resorted to intense mentor relationships for help at this point. To lay hold of the Dream and give it flesh was so difficult that they could not do it by themselves. Models and guides were needed—usually slightly older peers (not parents or parent surrogates) who were willing to foster the young adult's development "by believing in him, sharing the youthful dream and giving it his blessing."[10]

For a few men this Age Thirty Transition went smoothly, writes Levinson, but for the great majority this period was extremely stressful—like that of someone alone in the water between two islands, unable to move one way or the other and on the verge of drowning. A man's difficulties may be accentuated, he adds, "by specific aspects of his situation—economic recession, discrimination, the rivalries of a highly competitive world—and by his own emotional problems of committing himself to an occupation, relating to women and separating from parents."[11]

How might these insights be made fruitful in a study of Jesus' public mission? In earlier chapters we have come to see Jesus' baptism and temptations as a turning point during which he terminated an increasingly sterile role as surrogate "father" in his deceased father's family through a spiritual awakening and struggle. By means of this awakening and struggle he came to experience himself as "son" of a gracious heavenly father. With Erikson's and Levinson's outline before us of the generative and vocational urgencies typical of young men of this age group, it will be possible now, perhaps, to deepen our understanding of (1) why this experience opened up as it did (and as quickly as it did) into a forceful mission; (2) what it was that was central to that mission; and (3) how Jesus may have understood himself during this climactic phase of his life. It is to these three themes, then, that I will be turning in the remainder of this chapter, beginning with a second look at the transition from Jesus' hidden years to his public mission.

Jesus' "Age Thirty Transition"

To become a competent, "generative" individual for the average person is trial enough, but an achievement that nevertheless seems to emerge through a fairly coherent sequence of events. Childhood typically flows into adolescence without any great trauma, and adolescence into a growing sense of identity and competence. Marriage and parenthood follow, and in their wake the normal feelings of "care" that parents generally feel toward their families.

But the "great men" of history, when their lives are more fully known, frequently turn out to be extraordinary, not only at the point of their achievements, but also in the psychosocial developments that led to those achievements. For one thing, a longer and often more turbulent gestation period is required, it seems, for such men to "find themselves" and their true vocations. That Jesus spent his third decade in obscurity, working as a tradesman, is thus only what might be expected of someone who was destined to make an epochal contribution to humanity. During this same time in life, Luther was in a monastery, Freud was engaged in tedious anatomical research on eels, Darwin was on a five-year stint of botanical and biological investigation on board the *Beagle*, and Erikson himself (who more than anyone else has called these phenomena to our attention) was aimlessly wandering about Europe as a bohemian artist.

In each instance, this "moratorium," as Erikson has termed it, quite obviously served as an apprenticeship (or a trial run on being an adult, in Levinson's terms) during which competencies were acquired that, in retrospect, were vital to the later achievement. What these might have been in Jesus' case, in part at least, is not difficult to imagine. If it is true, as Buchanan has argued, that Jesus' work during his "hidden years" was more like that of a contractor (or construction engineer) than a village carpenter, then we would have to think of him as a businessman of sorts, managing others and traveling to nearby villages and cities (and to Sepphoris in particular, capital city of Galilee during Jesus' early years, and less than four miles from his home in Nazareth).[12] This picture of him would suggest that through his trade (and not just as head of his deceased father's family) Jesus not only acquired certain technical skills, but became adept in leadership and learned to know at first hand the people with whom and to whom he would later minister (tax collectors, merchants, fisherman and the like).

But this is not all. Even more important in the psychohistories of the greatest of the great are the *inner* struggles that typically preoccupy them during their "hidden" years—struggles that often turn out to have been related somehow to the most urgent psychological needs of their age. "An unrelenting determination" seems to be theirs, Richard Bushmann has written, "to settle psychological controversies which others experience but face less decisively."

> While most men conceal their anxieties and compromise rather than reconcile internal conflicts, an unusual integrity in the great man compels him to harmonize the warring elements. From his anguished quest for peace comes a new personal identity and with it a magnificent release of energy and determination. The combi-

> nation of a compelling new identity and individual magnetism galvanizes others and the great man, often without calculation, finds himself at the head of a movement.[13]

Freud may again be cited as an example. It was not only anatomical research that absorbed him during his moratorium but the origins of neurosis, and then increasingly the origins and healing of his own neurosis. This intensely personal search was foundational, as it turned out, both for his pioneering publication *The Interpretation of Dreams*, and his whole subsequent position in the psychoanalytic movement. Erikson too has given us a vivid account of the way his own struggle with identity-confusion during his twenties first led him to Freud and then to his important leadership role in the neo-Freudian enterprise in America.[14]

That difficult inner struggles of this nature may have also been a factor in Jesus' emergence as leader has already been intimated by what we have said regarding the possibility of his father's premature death and the associated emotional traumata. But we have said very little as yet concerning the way this crisis, and its resolution at the time of his baptism and temptations, may have been relevant to wider social and emotional problems of his age and hence to his mission. Striking evidence of this relevance is not lacking.

An especially important clue in this regard, I suggest, is the sometimes neglected report in John's Gospel that while still in Judea with John the Baptist (and hence relatively soon after his own baptism), Jesus himself began baptizing (John 3:22), and that as he did so, a remarkable thing suddenly happened. The crowds who had been going out to John now began turning to him, and in such numbers that it was reported that "all are going over to him" (John 3:26) and that he "was making and baptizing more disciples than John" (John 3:26).[15] In other words, at the very start of his evangelistic career, "without calculation," Jesus had become the "head of a movement." This phenomenon can only mean that in his case too there must have occurred an "anguished quest for peace" (to quote Bushmann again) that had proven to be relevant to problems that were troubling his contemporaries as well, and that the personal resolution he had arrived at (and which was now communicated by him) was immediately, intuitively recognized by many as meaningful.

Can we be more specific? I believe so, and especially if we recall once again that both John's mission and that of Jesus were attractive to quite discrete groups of people in Israel, and not to all. These were the Torah-disobedient "tax collectors and sinners" (as they are so often spoken of in the Gospels; see Mark 2:16; Matt. 11:19; Luke 15:1), as well as the Torah-ignorant and lax "common people" or *'am ha-aretz*, as they are referred to in talmudic sources (or the "poor" or "little ones" as Jesus preferred to call them; see Matt. 10:42; 11:5, 25; 18:10, 14; Mark 9:42; Luke 6:20).[16] In other words, it was not the bona fide members of the religious elite (Sadducees, Pharisees, Essenes, Scribes) who streamed out to John and to Jesus (Luke 7:29f.; Matt. 21:31f.) but *religious outsiders*—the "lost sheep of the house of Israel."

To understand why, we must say a little more regarding the emotional dilemma of this alienated sector of Palestinian Judaism. Their alienation was in part a reflex of what was happening among the religiously affiliated. According to Jacob Neusner, Jewish religious life in Palestine during this period was increasingly dominated by "lay people pretending to be priests" who were intent upon sanctifying daily life by treating "their homes as temples, and their tables as altars."[17] A fundamental conviction of these groups was that even those laws of the Pentateuch pertaining to the conduct and ritual purity of priests must be adhered to by all for *all* are God's people and should present themselves holy before God no matter where they lived.[18] The Synoptic Gospels themselves are replete with examples of the outcome of these beliefs. Washing rituals, food laws, tithing regulations, and rules for the Sabbath day came to occupy a place in religion on a par with foundational commandments like those of the decalogue (Luke 11:37-42; 18:12).

A great many in Israel, however, could not come to terms with this increasingly sacrist-nomistic form of religion.[19] These were not only the out and out sinners, but the previously referred to Torah-lax or ignorant *'am ha-aretz*, and the consequence of their noncompliance was not only that they must have felt themselves to be increasingly marginal to the religious life of their times, but that they were in some instances actively shunned and avoided by the religious elite.[20] What the emotional consequences of such ostracism for those being shunned might have been is not difficult to imagine. Their estrangement, confusion, and guilt over their religiously hopeless situation must, at times, have been overwhelming. Where could they turn? For the "lost" to find God is always difficult. Under these circumstances, it had become extremely so. As Marcus Borg has written, "both 'righteous' and 'sinners' would have internalized similar understandings of what it meant to be a faithful Jew" with the result that "the intensification of norms produced not only divisions within society, but also a large number of people who felt profoundly alienated and worthless."[21]

This feeling of estrangement is why, no doubt, John the Baptist found such an exuberant response among these masses, for he not only warned them of "wrath to come" but offered them a compellingly simple alternative: reconciliation with God on the basis of heartfelt repentance and a single baptism.[22] And this too, I now hypothesize, is one of the reasons why Jesus also was so attracted to him and why subsequent to his own baptism and temptations he was so warmly received among these same penitents—and even more warmly than John, as already intimated. For Jesus too offered them access to God through repentance and baptism, but we must now imagine (or how else could we explain his even greater evangelistic success?), with a deeper empathy, with even more integrity, with an even greater winsomeness.

Did his own prior experience of life have anything to do with this "plus" element in his mission? Having lost his father in adolescence, did he know how to "connect" with the "lost" to some special degree? Having had to wrestle with the pride, guilt, confusion, alienation, and doubt engendered by life in a "fatherless" world, did he feel even more deeply than John the predicament of his spiritually fatherless contemporaries? Was he, perhaps, for some period of his life, a disaffiliated *'am ha-aretz* himself, thus knowing from the inside what it was like to be cut off from the religious establishment and from God?[23] But having found God again, having experienced his forgiveness, having divested himself of his grandiosity (his temptations) and knowing now that this is not a fatherless world after all, could he not speak with a special clarity and "authority" (Mark 1:22) to the needs of these spiritually dispossessed?

It was clear to him now, in any case, what had to be done. Fresh from his baptismal experience, worldly-wise through his years as carpenter-contractor and custodian of his deceased father's family, inspired by the example of his newly-found mentor, John the Baptist, and above all, humbled and committed now to serving God and God only (and not Satan), he would follow in John's footsteps (and not return home). Like

John, he too would fast and pray and evangelize the masses who came out to them. Like John he too would bring about the purification and forgiveness of the guilty through water baptism (John 3:22), so that they might escape the coming "wrath" (Matt. 3:7//Luke 3:7).[24] John was the catalyst; Jesus' "hidden" years as head of his deceased father's family were the apprenticeship; his baptism and temptations were the turning point. Having left his parental home, having gone out to John, having himself had an experience of God's grace ("Thou art my beloved son . . .") and having broken free now of the satanic hubris that had so troubled him, he had at last "found himself" (Luke 15:17). Jesus was now poised and ready to fulfill *his* "Dream," to become at last the "generative man" God meant him to be.[25]

The Mission

It is well known, however, that Jesus did not remain long with John in Judea—not because of any falling out between them, but on account of John's tragic arrest and imprisonment (Mark 1:14; Luke 3:19f.), and the hostile pressures from the Scribal-Pharisaic establishment in Jerusalem which even then was carefully monitoring this possibly dangerous new movement (John 4:1).[26] It was at this time, the Gospels tell us, that he "withdrew" from Judea (Matt. 4:12) and began preaching the "good news" of God in his native Galilee (Mark 1:14).

There began that brief chapter of Jesus' life on which our Gospels focus almost exclusively. Needless to say, in discussing this portion of his life, it will be necessary (because of the fullness and complexity of these sources) to make a somewhat arbitrary selection of only the most relevant events and themes, our chief goal being to gain a general impression of the inner dynamics of the Jesus who confronts us at this climactic moment of his life.

On his own now in Galilee, and among his own, Jesus' whole mission (it would appear) took on a freer, more idiosyncratic style. For one thing, he ceased fasting, praying, and eating in the manner taught him by John (Matt. 9:14f.; 11:18f.; Luke 11:1). Nor do we read of him ever again baptizing.[27] Since these practices were essentials of John's program of purification for penitents (to escape the "wrath to come"), the fact that Jesus abandoned them at this point may be due to a uniquely personal "breakthrough" on his part with respect to how a person is made right with God (Luke 18:14).[28] It is not something *outside* a man "which by going into him can defile him," he began teaching (Mark 7:15), "since it enters, not his heart but his stomach, and so passes on" (Mark 7:19). "But the things which come out of a man [evil words and thoughts] are what defile him" (Mark 7:15, 19). It follows that a person's purification is also not accomplished through something external (ritual washings, or even outwardly flawless Torah-obedience), but through "cleansing those things which are within" (Luke 11:41) by heartfelt inner repentance (Luke 18:10-14), readiness to forgive (Matt. 18:23-35), compassion (Luke 10:29-37), and an unpretentious obedience to God (Luke 17:7-10) that attends to "the weightier matters of the law" (justice and mercy and faith) rather than its picayune details (Matt. 23:23).[29] It is for this reason, it seems, that he came to believe that wherever even the slightest turning to God and others occurs, there God is graciously present to forgive and heal, irrespective of the performance of purification rites, Sabbath rules, petty tithings, or the like.

Therefore, instead of waiting at one place (as John had done) for the "lost" to come to him, he went seeking them (Mark 1:38), and without fanfare or ritual, simply and directly, according to the requirements of each situation, ministered to their most basic needs—sometimes exorcising (Mark 1:25f.), sometimes healing (Mark 1:29-31), sometimes forgiving (Mark 2:5), sometimes forgiving *and* healing (Mark 2:10-12). Often astonishing things happened by means of a few simple words, so that people marveled at his authority (Mark 1:27; 2:12). Only too obviously, God's power was at work in and around him, a fact that he himself declared to be tangible evidence that God's kingdom is to be thought of not only as an event of the future (as it was for John the Baptist), but as a reality *already* manifesting itself "in the midst of" (and "within") those ready to receive it (Luke 17:20f.; 11:20; 19:9)—like leaven in dough (Matt. 13:33//Luke 13:20f.), or a budding fig tree in spring (Mark 13:28f.//Luke 21:29-31), or a tiny mustard seed falling to the ground and growing into a large branch (Mark 4:30-32).[30]

Thus it came about, as Borg summarizes, that Jesus began "speaking of a divine acceptance grounded in his own experience of God as merciful" and "began proclaiming a way of transformation that did not depend upon observing the requirements of the Torah as understood by [any of] the other renewal movements [of his time]."[31] The response of the disaffiliated masses (the *'am ha-aretz* and "sinners") was immediate. Large crowds were soon gathering wherever he went, so much so that he had to appoint "coworkers" to assist him in preaching, healing, and "reaping" this abundant "harvest," as he called it (Matt. 9:37; Luke 10:2).[32] What motivated him in doing so, we are told, was a wrenching sense of "compassion" for the crowds that were "harrassed and helpless like sheep without a shepherd" (Matt. 9:36), but that the number of those so appointed was "twelve" is also worth noting. It reveals an awareness now that what was unfolding was of significance not just for "the lost" but for "Israel" as a whole, and for the world at large.[33]

But as evangelistic success mounted, so did the opposition. The Scribal elite (both in Jerusalem and now in Galilee too) continued monitoring these astonishing developments (Luke 5:17), for what they observed was ominous from their point of view. Not only did Jesus do questionable things on the Sabbath (Mark 3:2; Luke 6:1f.), forgive sinners with an authority that belongs only to God (Mark 2:7), disregard the customary fasting and hand washing rituals (Mark 7:5), and teach in a manner that appeared to depreciate Torah (Mark 7:14-23), but even worse was the open manner in which he and his disciples fraternized with "sinners" (Mark 2:16). "Behold a glutton and drunkard, a friend of tax collectors and sinners!" was the opinion that spread (Matt. 11:19// Luke 7:34). As a result, he had to divert his energies from what had been to this point the primary focus of his mission—seeking and saving "the lost"—to defending his integrity and cause in the eyes of the religious elite. To do so, he resorted to simple, vivid, down-to earth stories through which he sought to bring about a recognition of the human naturalness and rationality of the approach he was taking and the dangers implicit in a too harsh, self-righteous attitude.[34] However, his defense, by and large, fell on deaf ears. In an alarmingly short time his mission among the "poor" and "the lost" was threatened by a plot among certain "Pharisees and Herodians" to "destroy him" (Mark 3:6).[35]

It was in the midst of these developments that disciples of John the Baptist arrived with the shattering news that their master was dead, beheaded by Herod Antipas (Matt. 14:12). Understandably, upon hearing it, Jesus once again "withdrew" (Matt. 14:13). At the time of John's imprisonment, he had withdrawn to continue his mission elsewhere, but this time, he withdrew to find solitude. Clearly John's death affected him deeply, and he had come to a turning point.[36] His choice was either to abandon his mission in order to escape the dangers that now threatened everywhere, or to press forward whatever the consequences. His decision was to press forward, "for," he said, "whoever would save his life will lose it, but whoever loses his life for my sake and the Gospel will save it" (Mark 8:35). He subsequently left Galilee (Mark 7:24), initially moving northward to regions beyond Herod's control (diminishing thereby the possibility of being arrested and imprisoned as John was), and then headed southward "through Galilee" (Mark 9:30) into Judea and on up to Jerusalem itself.

Increasingly on his mind now, obviously, was not only the salvation of "sinners" but the fate of his people and the world. What troubled him, more specifically, it seems, was the possibility that the harsh, self-righteous attitudes of the religious elite would not only alienate the "poor" and undermine their status with God but intensify the already mounting tensions with Rome (and with Gentiles generally) and bring about a catastrophic war (Luke 13:1-5). Earlier he had addressed this issue with unprecedented words about loving as God loves, good and bad alike, even those who mistreat and persecute you (Matt. 5:43-48; Luke 6:27-36). But as he approached Jerusalem on his last journey and crossed the hills overlooking the city from the east, amidst the ecstasy and jubilation of his disciples he wept, because of his premonition of the inevitability of just such a devastating invasion due to the fact that its leaders did not know "the things that make for peace" (Luke 19:37-44).[37]

On the following day he went to the temple and drove out those who bought and sold there, declaring as he did so: "Is it not written, 'My house shall be called a house of prayer for all the nations'? But you have made it a den of robbers" (Mark 11:17). Borg thinks this action was a prophetic protest against the way the temple had become a focal point of militant separatist tendencies.[38] But his words about the house of God becoming "a house of prayer for all nations" suggest that foremost on his mind now was his people's ancient hopes of this temple being one day a place of pilgrimage for peoples worldwide (Isa. 2:1-5; 56:1-7; Jer. 3:14-17; Zech. 8:20-23). Indeed, even earlier he had envisioned just such an influx of Gentiles from east and west and north and south to "sit at table with Abraham, Isaac and Jacob in the kingdom of heaven" (Matt.

8:11//Luke 13:29).[39] Meyer believes that a riddle spoken at this time alluding to the destruction and reconstruction of the temple "in three days" (Mark 14:58//Matt. 26:61//John 2:18-20) is further evidence of his certainty now that the "gratuitous reign of God" so manifest during his mission was about to become powerful (despite the opposition) in the wider world through his sacrificial death and the events transpiring in its wake (Mark 10:45; 14:24f.).[40]

While many heard him gladly, to the authorities he was only another dangerous troublemaker who would need to be silenced if public peace were to be maintained.[41] On the night before Passover, therefore (John 13:1), fully aware now of the forces ranged against him, he gathered his inner circle of disciples for what he knew would be his last meal.[42] "I tell you that from now on," he is quoted as saying, "I shall not drink of the fruit of the vine until the kingdom of God comes" (Luke 22:18). After requesting that his disciples remember him and what he stood for, and a final hymn (Mark 14:22-26), he spent an agonizing night in prayer preparing for the ordeal of the coming day (Mark 14:34-36). At dawn he was arrested, tried, and charged with blasphemy for not having denied he was the Messiah and for saying he would soon be "seated at the right hand of the power of God" (Luke 22:69//Matt. 26:64).[43] At noon on Passover Preparation Day (John 19:14) he was put to death.

"Who do men say that I am?"

In the light of all that has been learned about him in our inquiry so far, how shall we characterize Jesus in this final momentous chapter of his life? What manner of man was he, and what, essentially, was he trying to accomplish?

What has long puzzled interpreters (both ancient and modern) as they have struggled with these questions is the degree to which Jesus' words and actions during this phase of his mission are unique and difficult to capture within any of the traditional roles or stereotypes. Hengel writes that he appears to have "stood outside *any discoverable teaching tradition of Judaism*."[44] He is definitely a "holy man" of sorts with something prophet-like about him (Mark 6:4; 8:27; Luke 13:32), but his language is predominantly that of a man of wisdom and ripe experience.[45] Thoughts of the Messiah come to mind in his presence, yet when pressed to declare himself as such, he is evasive (Matt. 11:2-6; Mark 8:30; Matt. 26:64; Mark 15:2). He is ideologically, vocationally, and emotionally close to John the Baptist, but after John's arrest and the transfer of his mission to Galilee, he seems to be increasingly his own man.

This latter observation may in fact have been true in a more profound sense than is generally recognized and may afford us an important clue to the enigma we are talking about. Common to identity formation in young adulthood (and the Age Thirty Transition) is the role of a mentor or guide with whom an emotional bond is formed. Gradually, however (sometimes rather quickly), the intensity of this bond diminishes as the individual reinvests his newly won self-understanding with insights and gifts of his own. Wilhelm Fliess, a Berlin physician, played this role for Freud, as we know from their lively, intimate correspondence.[46] Freud in turn served in a similar fashion in Erikson's identity formation.[47] Both men, after intense involvement with these "mentors," as we might call them, moved on to become distinguished leaders in their own right. In a similar fashion, we might imagine, Jesus too, after identifying with John, increasingly differentiated himself in the months following John's arrest. He was free now to go his own way, think his own thoughts, do his own deeds. His return to his native Galilee may be viewed as a first step in this process. It is indeed, then, no stereotype that confronts us in the records of this period, but an increasingly individualized Jesus with his own unique sense of calling and vision.[48]

But what calling, more specifically, and what vision? Granted his uniqueness and the difficulty of capturing his identity in any of the traditional categories, how *shall* we characterize the Jesus we encounter in the records of this moment of his life?

That Jesus himself on one occasion self-consciously raised a question of this nature is, to say the least, striking, and merits our attention first of all. "Who do men say that I am?" he is reported to have asked his disciples at Caesarea Philippi, shortly before he began that fateful last journey to Jerusalem referred to above. And then he asked, "But who do you say that I am?" (Mark 8:27-29). The very questions testify to a certain preoccupation at this stage of his career with self-identity issues. What others were saying about him, what his disciples thought of him, was, it seems, a crucial matter. And yet, as we discover from the disciples' answers and his response, this concern was not because of some neurotic fascination with his own importance, for according to our oldest source (Mark), Peter's ecstatic "You are the Christ!" was greeted by him not with an approving: "Blessed are you . . ." (as in Matt. 16:17) but with a stern warning to "tell no one" (Mark 8:30) and then a sharp, emotional rejoinder (when Peter persisted in his messianic projection): "Get behind me, Satan! For you are not on the side of God, but of men" (Mark 8:33). It would appear, therefore, that he asked his disciples who they thought he was, *not* (as traditionally thought) to *elicit* a messianic confession of faith on their part, but just the opposite. He wanted his disciples' incipient messianic idealizations brought to light so that they could be dealt with openly and quashed. It follows that a continuing feature of Jesus' self-identity at this culminating stage of his life was a highly emotional abhorrence and rejection of the prevailing grandiose messianic stereotype, precisely as at the time of his temptations. To be thought of in those terms (or so to think of himself), he declared, was satanic, godless, and utterly human (on the side of men, not of God).[49]

That a conviction of this nature was in fact at the core of Jesus' inner world at this time is further indicated by the report of his response to an inquiry regarding this very issue by his former mentor, John the Baptist (Matt. 11:4-6//Luke 7:18-23). John, we are told, was in prison at the time, but reports had apparently come to him of what his protege was now saying and doing. These may have quickened earlier messianic premonitions on his part regarding Jesus. And yet, for whatever reason, there were also doubts.[50] John therefore dispatched two disciples to confront Jesus directly and settle the matter one way or the other: "Are you he who is to come, or shall we look for another?" (Matt. 11:3//Luke 7:19).

Jesus' reply (more accurately preserved in Matthew than in Luke) begins with a poetic allusion to the age of salvation: "Go and tell John . . . the blind receive their sight and the lame walk . . . and the poor have good news preached to them" (Matt. 11:4f.).[51] It concludes with an indirect appeal that John not be offended by the course his mission has taken: "Blessed is he who takes no offense at me" (Matt. 11:6). This suggests that Jesus was quite aware now of having deviated from John's program. He knows that what he has just said might well offend John (as much as he wishes it would not), for John had prophesied of "One to come" who would bring about a forceful separation between wheat and chaff and baptize with "spirit and fire" (Matt. 3:11f.//Luke 3:16f.), whereas in Jesus' answer to John's inquiry he had spoken only of healing and "good news for the poor." His reply must therefore be viewed as a signal to John that even though he still shared John's conviction that an age of salvation was dawning, he in no way wanted to be thought of as John's magisterial "coming One." Indeed, it would seem that by this point in Jesus' mission, John's messianic expectations had lost a good bit of their relevance for him for not only does Jesus sidestep John's question on this occasion, but later when teaching his disciples a prayer (Luke 11:1) he refers not at all to the coming of a purifying messianic Baptizer but only to the coming of God's kingdom (Luke 11:2).[52]

But if not that, what then? If "Messiah" as imagined by his disciples and John signified, so to speak, the negative, dark side of Jesus' identity, the side he wished to reject and suppress, how, in a more positive sense, *did* he think of himself? Virtually everything Jesus said or did, of course, bears ultimately on this question, but contemporary scholarship has progressively centered upon an ecstatic saying of his (spoken, we are told, in the heat of his Galilean mission) as of very special relevance to this question. It is one that begins with an exuberant word of thanks to the "Father, Lord of heaven and earth," for the "fullness" (Greek: *panta*) of the things that were being "revealed" through him to "babes" (Matt. 11:25//Luke 10:21)—"yes, Father, for such was your gracious will" (Matt. 11:26//Luke 10:21). This "fullness" of revelation, he went on to explain (Matt. 11:27//Luke 10:22), was one that had been given him by his Father and could be likened to the knowledge a caring father has of a son, and a son of his father—"and any one to whom the Son chooses to reveal him."[53] Especially notable here is the emotional quality of these words. They alert us to the passion with which Jesus felt himself at this moment of his life to be the prophetic mediator of an embracing "revelation" of God as gracious father. When, therefore, elsewhere in his teachings we encounter repeated references to God's radiant fatherly love for good and bad alike (Matt. 5:45), for the birds of the air and the flowers of the field (Matt. 6:26-32//Luke 12:24-28), for the lost (Luke 15:20-24) and those who need "rest" for their souls (Matt. 11:29f.), then, it should be clearer to us, in this light, that these convictions were more than ideas—but deeply felt existential certainties. Above everything else, they seemingly are what filled his consciousness at this climactic stage of his career.[54]

It is understandable, therefore, that hard evidence that he appropriated to himself any titles or dignities of a more fixed or stereotypical nature (as once thought) is proving to be increasingly elusive.[55] Precisely because God's goodness was so real to him, human adulation was suspect ("Why do you call me good? No one is good but God alone"; Mark 10:18) and honorific titles abhorrent ("But you are not to be called rabbi, for you have one teacher. . . . And call no man your father on earth, for you have one Father. Neither be called masters, for you have one master"; Matt. 23:8-10).[56] It is also fully consistent with this that as his mission neared its end, he is said to have begun teaching that true greatness lies not in being domineering or controlling (as is the practice among Gentile rulers), but in love for God and others (Mark 12:29f.) actualized through humble service (Mark 10:42-45; Matt. 20:25-28; 23:11f.; Luke 22:27).[57]

There are, however, two additional facets of Jesus' activity at this stage of his life that merit some attention if his "Age Thirty" identity is to be understood as fully as it might be. Often, we are told, when uncertain about what to do next in his mission, he would withdraw into solitude for prayer (Mark 1:35; Luke 6:12, 46; 14:32-43),[58] and when challenged by the religious elite to give an account of himself concerning that most crucial aspect of his mission, his association with sinners (Luke 15:1f.), he replied not with citations from Scripture or tradition, but with down-to-earth stories about people and events drawn from the daily life of Palestine. Both his manner of praying and his parables, I suggest, testify to a highly individual and *personal* process of working out the specifics of his identity and mission. In existential dialogue with his spiritual Father and through astute reflection on the realities of daily life as he experienced them, there came to him, it seems, those concrete images and models for being what he was and doing what he did that repeatedly occur in the stories he told. From them we learn that his "role models" were not predominantly the great men of history (whether scriptural or secular) but a shepherd searching for a lost sheep (Luke 15:4-7), a father rejoicing at the return of a lost son (Luke 15:11-32), a vineyard owner paying out a day's wage to all his workers regardless of how long they had worked (Matt. 20:1-16), a despised Samaritan stopping and stooping (after others had passed by) to assist a man wounded by robbers (Luke 10:29-37), a great king not ruling in the usual sense, but forgiving the hopelessly large debt of one of his underlings (Matt. 18:23-35).

Through these and many another earthy contemporary figure and scene, Jesus not only defended his mission but made transparent his own wise shepherd-like, father-like, Samaritan-like feelings of generative compassion and care.[59]

Earlier in our inquiry (chap. 4) these same stories were referred to as evidence of Jesus' positive attitude toward father-figures. I noted that in his winsome portrayal of these uniformly strong, competent, in-charge, yet peculiarly forgiving and compassionate men we can catch a glimpse of how he felt about people in roles of this kind. Here, as our study draws to a close, I cite them again, but this time as prime evidence of how he must have felt about himself as well. If at the Jordan, as earlier suggested, Jesus found his "father" again, and a renewed sense of sonship, then now during his "age thirty" mission to the "lost sheep of the house of Israel," he found himself as well. And it was an identity not unlike that of the Father he now served. "Be merciful," he once said to his disciples, "even as your Father is merciful" (Luke 6:36). Just such an *Imitatio Dei*—the embodiment of God's generative care and graciousness in the nitty-gritty of daily life—was, it seems, the reality that more than anything else engaged him at this climactic stage of his life.[60]

9

Jesus at Thirty

The true saints are those who transfer the state of householdership to the house of God, becoming father and mother, brother and sister, son and daughter, to all creation, rather than to their own issue.[1]

The Man Who Emerges

The task remaining in this final chapter is to reflect briefly on a few of the highlights of the picture of Jesus that have emerged in the preceding inquiry. In doing so, I have found provocative a comment of Erik Erikson's regarding an aspect of the life of the great Indian leader Mohandas Gandhi. In his book *Gandhi's Truth*, Erikson conjectures that had Gandhi not lived in a culture in which child marriages were customary, he might have chosen as a young adult to remain celibate. In that case, he says, one can imagine him becoming a famous monk, perhaps, but hardly the national leader and reformer who succeeded so magnificently in transferring the state of his "householdership" from wife and children to the urgent needs of India at the time of its struggle for independence. And to do that, Erikson declares, is the mark of a "true saint."[2]

From our study it would appear that Jesus too, as a young adult, was involved in an analogous transfer of "householdership" (or "generativity" as Erikson has also termed it). In any case, it will be remembered, that our inquiry began (in chap. 2) by observing the gulf that had opened up between Jesus and his biological family at the beginning of his public mission, and was concluded (in chap. 8) with an analysis of the way in which, at that same time, he was moved by compassion for the distraught and suffering "lost sheep of the house of Israel." That these two realities—detaching from his family of origins and his mission of mercy on behalf of these "lost"—were related somehow in Jesus' own mind seems evident from his striking words about his family being not those who are such by ties of blood, but those related by their common bond with a merciful God (Mark 3:34f.). If Erikson is right that "the true saints are those who transfer the state of householdership to the house of God, becoming father and mother, brother and sister, son and daughter to all creation, rather than to their own issue" only,[3] then surely Jesus must be ranked among them.

But in what sense, in his case, is it possible to speak of a transfer of *householdership?* If Jesus was celibate (as generally assumed), and therefore without a household or family of his own (unlike Gandhi), then it would appear he had little or no experience of "householdership" to transfer. But then too it would be difficult to know how to account for his extraordinary giftedness at thirty for down-to-earth, father-like wisdom and compassion, and the unique efflorescence of this in his public mission. However, if it is true that his father had died prematurely, then even though unmarried himself, Jesus would have been no stranger to the complex task of heading up a family, for inevitably upon him, as eldest son, would have fallen the demanding responsibilities of surrogate "husband" and "father" in the family of his widowed mother. Thus, in the developmental background of Jesus there might have been an experience of "householdership" after all, one, in fact, precociously thrust upon him and hence of more than ordinary intensity.

The gradual surfacing of this possibility and the light it sheds on the personality of the thirty-year-old Jesus may be one of the more seminal findings of this inquiry. It has offered us, first of all, a compelling alternative perspective on his celibacy. Neither personal nor vocational necessities on his part appear to have been the precipitating reasons for this, but cultural expectations and forces that came into play as a consequence of his father's premature death. For it was the father in that society who was charged with finding a wife for his son, but tradition dictated that if he died before having done so, the eldest son should take his place in the care of the family left behind—a circumstance bound to modify or delay the son's plans for marriage and founding a family of his own.

The possibility that in Jesus' case this is what happened has also afforded us another way of viewing the domestic crisis that captured our attention at the very outset of our study: Jesus' estrangement from his family of origins at the beginning of his mission. Few situations in life are as emotionally complex and wrenching as that of a son caught up in the necessity of assuming his father's role with his own mother. If she at this time of his life was mystified by his sudden shift in loyalty from her and her family to "God's family," and thought momentarily that her son was "beside himself" and in need of restraint (Mark 3:21, 33), we must conclude that she, like many mothers in her predicament, was more attuned to her own needs and necessities than to his.

Against this backdrop of his father's death and Jesus' subsequent role as breadwinner and guardian of his father's family, many another facet of his emotionality becomes luminous as well: his fierce battle with "satanic" hubris (the psychological after-effects of a precocious assumption of his deceased father's role); his "Age Thirty Transition" and baptism at the Jordan (where he humbled himself and experienced God as gracious Father); his emotional bonding with John the Baptist (a surrogate father and mentor for Jesus in this crucial transitional period of his life); his joyful creativity and courage (after John's arrest) in his own new-found "calling" as "generative" prophet-evangelist of God's love for the "lost" (a father now himself with a "family" of his own, one "born not of blood nor of the will of the flesh nor of the will of man, but of God," John 1:13); his extraordinary faith and intuitively wise "father-like" talent for relating helpfully to all types of people and situations (the fruit in part, no doubt, of an emotionally secure childhood and his years of leadership in his deceased father's family).

"Tempted as we are"

In this light too the somewhat troublesome questions sometimes posed regarding the mental and emotional health of the thirty-year-old Jesus can be freshly addressed (see the Appendix). Psychiatrists and psychologists who early in this century raised questions about his "sanity" because of studies then appearing that portrayed him as having had an inflated messianic view of himself were not without warrant, for it is common knowledge that delusions of grandeur and fantasies of power are symptomatic of disturbed states of mind. But what has also become apparent through this inquiry is that the Jesus of history during his public mission was fiercely opposed to such thoughts, both within himself and his culture—and that he was eminently successful in this so far as his own self-identity was concerned. As an early Christian poet put it, "he humbled himself and became obedient unto death . . ." (Phil. 2:8).[4]

Yet signs and symptoms of the struggle involved are also evident. He does not seem to have "found himself" until relatively late in life, and even then it was by means of a conversion-type experience characteristic of those who must suffer considerable emotional turmoil before reaching maturity. The "conversion" itself, it appears, orbited around "sonship" and culminated in a battle with "Satan" during which, though victorious, Jesus was sorely tested. Such "testings," we now know, are a recurrent feature of the inner world of men and women of high achievement. Pope John XXIII, for example, one of the humblest of twentieth-century leaders, wrote in his posthumously published *Journal of a Soul* of the "fantastic dreams" of "positions and honours" that afflicted him all his life.[5] His "enemy within," he called them. "In the end," he said, "I was able to get the better of it. But I was mortified to feel it constantly returning."[6]

A similar struggle marked the early years of the world-famous martyr-theologian Dietrich Bonhoeffer, according to a carefully researched psychohistorical study. We are told that he initially embraced theology itself as a tactic for surpassing his prestigious father and brothers.[7] In a memoir written when he was twenty-six, Bonhoeffer himself tells of the "contemptible vanity" that plagued him in doing so. "How often," he lamented, "he had sought to master it [his vanity]. But it always crept back again and . . . forced an entry into the house of his soul and made him afraid."[8] Only through a deep-going conversion to the God of the Bible and to Jesus was he finally released from this agonizing state of mind. He went on to discover that human strength touched by humility can be authentically given in the service of others. At this juncture of his life, his biographer tells us, he at last felt ready for "a venture in intimacy he had never made before."[9] He became engaged. But, as with Jesus, marriage eluded him, for he was already implicated in those activities against Hitler that would quickly lead to his imprisonment and death.

Not all who are troubled in this manner succeed in surmounting their "temptations." Hitler may be cited as an example of someone who, beset by similar grandiose compulsions, not only yielded, but in yielding brought the world with him to the brink of destruction.[10] It would appear that the great men who fail in this crucial confrontation with hubris may descend to the depths and become the tragic anti-Christs of history, while those who instead humble themselves are the pillars upon whom whatever sanity the world has is continually being built and rebuilt.

He was "in every respect tempted as we are, yet without sin." That was the opinion regarding the psyche of Jesus of the unknown author of the Letter to the Hebrews (4:15). What finally is ours? If "without sin" may be taken to mean that he emerged from his developmental trials "victoriously," then my conclusion, in any case, would have to be similar. Growing up as he did in a troubled family (bereft of its father) and a troubled time (bereft of its God), Jesus must have indeed been sorely and persistently "tempted." That he faced and surmounted these trials and emerged from them a gifted yet humble "evangelist" of God's love—and that he did this with such intelligence, realism, insight, artistry, and courage (and at such a critical juncture in the life of his people and the world) that his achievement can still be meaningful twenty centuries later—is an impression that has grown steadily stronger in the course of this inquiry.[11]

Appendix

The Psychological Study of Jesus: A Review and Critique of the Discussion to Date

> *Should it really turn out that Jesus' object world must be considered by the doctor as in some degree the world of a sick man, still this conclusion, regardless of the consequences that follow from it and the shock to many that would result from it, must not remain unuttered, since reverence for truth must be exalted above everything else.*[1]

Initial Questions

When launching a fresh study of an old issue, it is always important to know what may have already been said about it. The emotionality of Jesus truly is such an issue, with a history stretching back to the lifetime of Jesus himself (Mark 3:21). It was not, however, until the rise of modern historical and psychological research in the nineteenth and early twentieth centuries that this topic came forward in anything like a focused way. Since then it has never entirely left us. Even historical Jesus studies with an explicitly antipsychological bias inevitably focus on one facet or another of his personality, and in doing so make him vulnerable to psychological inquiry.[2]

In a sense, then, a really comprehensive survey of the way Jesus has been understood psychologically would require that we review the entire history of historical Jesus research.[3] That would, of course, take us far beyond what is possible here or needed for the topic at hand. It will be enough for our purposes if we can highlight some of the more significant episodes in this quest, especially those in which the psychology of Jesus was investigated in a more or less direct and self-conscious way.

With that goal in mind, there is little doubt as to where we should begin. Something must be said, first of all, about the controversy at the beginning of this century over the possibility that Jesus at thirty, far from being a model of emotional health, may in fact have suffered from a mental illness of some sort.[4] In this debate some of the more important psychological observations surfaced which even today cause us a certain amount of perplexity.

Preparing the way for this discussion were the historical Jesus studies referred to earlier, for the immediate effect of these was to highlight the novelty of Jesus' messianic self-understanding. So long as Jesus was viewed within the framework of the historic confessions of the church, his messianic identity was thought of as nothing more than one might expect. As soon as Jesus began to be studied historically, however, his self-identity at thirty became a problem. How could a supposedly sensible and good man entertain such patently grandiose ideas about himself?

One of the first to feel the weight of this question and write about it was David Friedrich Strauss, whose *Leben Jesu* (1835) was to become one of the landmark studies of modern times.[5] In the initial edition of his book, Strauss concluded that although many facets of Jesus' life as portrayed in the canonical Gospels were mythic and hence nonhistorical, there is no reason to doubt that already the Jesus of history had actually thought of himself as the future-coming Son of Man spoken of in Daniel and hence as someone who would soon appear on the clouds of heaven to judge the world and establish God's kingdom. But if that were the case, Strauss pondered, what judgment is one compelled to make about his mental health?

Initially he tried to defend Jesus by suggesting that even an idea as extravagant as this one, "in a nation segregated by the peculiarities of its faith . . . if only it were consistent and had, in some of its aspects, truth and dignity, might allure even a reasonable man beneath its influence."[6] Later on, however, he wrote to his friend Wilhelm Lang:

> The hard nut of the second coming was too difficult for me; I have not been able to swallow it. I find in the earlier sayings of Jesus, above all the sermon on the Mount, so rational a tendency that I cannot properly credit him with an idea that in my view lies so close to insanity.[7]

Consequently, Strauss went on to produce a second version of the life of Jesus, this one written for a popular audience (*Das Leben Jesu für das deutsche Volk bearbeitet*, 1864), in which he modified the earlier picture of Jesus, describing him now as "a religious genius" who spoke of the future, but not of his own second coming.[8]

Once raised, however, the question of Jesus' "sanity" could not so easily be put aside, and Ernst Renan's *La Vie de Jesus* (1863), with its references to Jesus' "singular taste for persecution" (as he approached the end of his life) and his "fearful increase of enthusiasm," did little to dispel it.[9]

It was not, however, until the opening decade of the twentieth century that this theme began to surface in a serious way. Two parallel developments seem to have provided the final impetus. On the one hand, psychiatry was now increasingly intent upon classifying the various mental illnesses and linking them with their imagined neurological origins. This growing fund of knowledge, as it was supposed, was then applied not only to the treatment of the mentally ill, but to the analysis of certain "great men" of history whose lives, it was observed, were frequently (and rather mysteriously) marred by symptoms of mental illnesses of one kind or another ("superior degenerates," Moebius called them).[10]

At the same time, after several decades of rationalistic reinterpretations of Jesus' life, a more disciplined, scientific study of the Gospels seemed to be confirming the picture of Jesus drawn earlier by Strauss in his initial *Leben Jesu* of 1835. A masterful study by Johannes Weiss, *Die Predigt Jesu vom Reich Gottes* (1892), was particularly influential in this respect. Here Weiss argued convincingly that Jesus, far from being a modern man of "reason," believed that the world was about to be transformed by God and that he himself would participate in this cataclysm, first of all by suffering an atoning death for the world's sins, and then by returning as "Son of Man" to judge the nations and rule over God's kingdom.[11] Albert Schweitzer had independently arrived at similar conclusions about Jesus in a brilliantly written critique of the prior century of historical Jesus research, *Von Reimarus zu Wrede* (1908).[12] Given this portrait and the prevailing psychiatric point of view, it is not surprising that Jesus too would eventually become the focus of psychiatric observation and debate.

The debate began in earnest in 1905 with a publication entitled *Jesus Christus vom Standpunkte des Psychiaters*. Its author was Dr. George Lomer, the head physician of an institute for the insane in Neustadt, Germany, although he wrote under a pseudonym (Dr. George de Loosten).[13] Here he proposed that Jesus was probably a neurological "degenerate" by birth and may have, quite early in his youth, attracted attention to himself because of his pronounced self-consciousness and meagerly developed sense of family and sex. This conclusion, Lomer emphasized, should not detract from our appreciation of Jesus' accomplishments. He was only too obviously a figure of great intelligence who was able to recognize the mistakes in the prevailing religious conceptions of his time. Above all, he gave the precepts of the law an interpretation that was new in form, freer and more capable of development, and thus launched a religious revolution. In the end, however, it was his neurological illness that gained the upper hand and precipitated a fixed system of delusions, the particulars of which were determined by the intense religious bent of his age and his own one-sided preoccupation with the Scriptures of the Old Testament.

In a psychopathological study of Jesus that appeared in the same year (1905),[14] the Danish scholar Emil Rasmussen noted a similar set of symptoms. He, too, felt that a medical diagnosis was required. Jesus, like many another religious prophet (Buddha, Paul, Mohammad), he wrote, exhibits all the symptoms of "epilepsy."

An American medical specialist, William Hirsch, joined the discussion in 1912 with still another clinical diagnosis: "paranoia."[15] By this he referred to a mental degeneracy characterized by delusions of persecution or grandeur, or both. Hirsch speculated that the problem in Jesus' case may have been rooted in a hereditary disposition but was decidedly aggravated by an early overly zealous study of the Scriptures, which he later (in a typically paranoid manner) referred to himself. It was another paranoiac, John the Baptist, who by announcing the coming of a Messiah precipitated the baptismal hallucinations that convinced Jesus that he was God's son. From that point on, Jesus developed a progressive megalomania. "All his speeches, doctrines, and sermons culminated in the one word 'I.' I am the King of Heaven, I am the Saviour of man, I am the son of God, I and God are one . . . , I, and always I . . . [and] hatred towards anyone who does not agree with him in everything. . . ."[16]

During the years 1910–1915, a French professor of psychology, Charles Binet-Sanglé, added yet another four volumes to the discussion. Their collective title was *La Folie de Jesus*, and he, like Hirsch, thought Jesus' problem to be "paranoia" of a religious type.[17] The preaching of John the Baptist, the response of the crowds to his miracles, the enthusiasm of the disciples—all conspired to give Jesus the idea that he was God's Messiah, and indeed one with God himself. Even the Pharisees played a role in the formation of his delusional system. Through their hostility they planted the notion that he would have to die for the sins of the nation, after which he would be resurrected, ascend into the heavens, and from there be revealed.

Albert Schweitzer

Both the public and scholarly response to these and other publications of the kind were less than one might have expected. As of 1922, apart from short periodical reviews, Walter Bundy (who undertook to survey the literature on this issue to that date) was able to identify only four separately published replies, all of them pamphlets.[18]

The best known of these in the English-speaking world was Albert Schweitzer's essay *Die psychiatrische Beurteilung Jesus*, written initially as a thesis in fulfillment of the requirements for a medical degree, and first published in 1913.[19] Schweitzer felt that he was partly responsible for the growing number of negative psychiatric opinions about Jesus that were appearing, because of conclusions, as noted, that he himself had published. He was all the more concerned, therefore, to exonerate Jesus, for whom he still had the deepest respect.

And this he tried to do, first of all, by calling Jesus' psychiatric critics to task for their uncritical use of the Gospel sources, above all their reliance on the Gospel of John. He also charged them with a lack of appreciation for the milieu in which Jesus grew up and lived. Jesus was, after all, a child of late Judaism sharing fully in its apocalyptic expectations. In that environment his messianic consciousness must be judged far differently than it would be in ours. Even his lack of family loyalty can be accounted for,

Schweitzer maintained, by the "peculiar preconceptions" of his time (although he failed to specify what these might have been).

Schweitzer did concede, however, that even with these considerations in mind, "the very fact that he [Jesus] regarded himself as the man who would enter upon the supernatural inheritance of the family of David, remains still a striking thing."[20] Nevertheless, a judgment that this was something sick or morbid, Schweitzer argued, would only be possible if it could be shown that it was part of a more comprehensive disease process in which ideas of injury and persecution were in evidence as well. Schweitzer was convinced that this was not the case. "Jesus had, indeed, enemies and opponents," he wrote, "because he spoke out against the narrow-minded and external piety of the Pharisees. [But] in relation to these opponents, not imaginary but genuine, Jesus conducts himself in a fashion diametrically opposite to the conduct of a sick man with a persecutory trend. He does not remain inactive and does not limit himself to a defensive attitude like so many of the sick who believe themselves persecuted."[21] Since there is no evidence of a "persecution complex" in Jesus, Schweitzer concluded, there is no basis either for raising questions about his sanity.

At this point, however, Schweitzer was on shaky ground, as Winfred Overholser pointed out in the foreword to the English edition of Schweitzer's book. "Some paranoids manifest ideas of grandeur almost entirely," Overholser wrote, "and we find patients whose grandeur is very largely of a religious nature, such as their belief that they are directly instructed by God to convert the world or perform miracles."[22] In other words, religious grandiosity of the kind attributable to Jesus may be a symptom of emotional disturbance, in and of itself.

Thus, the "Jesus sanity" debate can be said to have ended in a stalemate. Textual and psychiatric data presented themselves that neither side knew what to do with. Jesus' apparently grandiose self-identity proved to be an especially thorny issue, as were his attitudes toward sex and family. Suspicions of a problem of one kind or another were not without reason, nor were the attempted diagnoses, although Schweitzer was certainly correct in calling for a more careful use of the sources.

Above all, it must be noted that both sides were locked into an inadequate "disease-model" of mental illness. Symptoms were studied with a view to proving or disproving a possible "neurological degeneracy." If

Jesus were in fact suffering from a mental disorder, it was assumed that this had little bearing on other facets of his life or achievement. As a consequence it was difficult, if not impossible, to convey a really satisfying impression of Jesus in his wholeness. Further progress would have to wait for someone who had broken free of this "myth of mental illness" and could read the data of Jesus' life in the light of a more dynamic psychology.

Anton Boisen

That someone was Anton Boisen, whose pioneering studies in religion and mental illness are still waiting to be fully appreciated. In a 1936 publication, *The Exploration of the Inner World*, Boisen picked up the discussion of Jesus' psyche where Schweitzer had left it.[23] He noted Schweitzer's insistence that Jesus did indeed think of himself as Messiah, but that this is no reason to judge him mentally ill. Boisen, who himself experienced several psychotic episodes, agreed with Schweitzer on the first point but not on the second. In his professional role as chaplain in a mental hospital he initiated research into the religious thought-world of the mentally ill and discovered that feelings of standing on the brink of a world catastrophe, of being the long-awaited Messiah, of being charged with a mission, of the necessity of self-sacrifice, of death and rebirth, and of being in direct communication with God are recurrent among hospitalized patients. It cannot be denied, Boisen argued, that Jesus also had such thoughts. But neither should it be denied that in his case too these might well have been symptomatic of mental illness. The issue is not *whether* Jesus suffered in this way. That is only too evident. The issue is *what* he did with this crisis of his life.

Boisen was convinced, both from personal experience and on the basis of his research, that many forms of mental illness are not "illness" in the usual sense of that word. They are emotional upheavals precipitated more often than not by urgent, unresolved personal and moral conflicts. The grandiose feelings, the fear of cosmic catastrophe, the confrontation with death and with mission are not manifestations of organic "degeneracy," but of *inner* struggles.

> The individual here stands face to face with the great realities of death and life, of personal destiny in success and failure, and with the social whole to which he gives allegiance. The experience itself is essentially a withdrawal into the solitude of the inner world for the purpose of getting clear on the central objectives and thus getting a new start in life.[24]

The outcome of such a struggle is not inevitable. Many back off from the moral challenge and retreat permanently into a world of psychotic fantasy. In Boisen's view, Jesus is a supreme example of someone who faced the challenge, suffered through the chaotic ordeal, and emerged victorious. "The significance of Jesus would then be found precisely in the fact that, passing through this most searching experience, he came forth unscathed and achieved the highest degree of social harmony not only in his inner organization but in his social perspective."[25]

In making these suggestions, Boisen opened a new window into the inner world of Jesus at thirty. "He was tempted in all points as we are," Boisen said in effect. His claim to our allegiance is not that he was without problems, but that he faced these problems and emerged from them more mature, more capable of serving his age and the ages since.

But what actually were his problems? If afflicted, how? If triumphant, in what sense? Boisen's answer was that so far as Jesus was concerned, the inner crisis was not precipitated by a *moral* conflict, as is usually the case, but by an intense emotional identification on his part with the fate of his nation. But would this precipitate a mental illness of the type and magnitude Boisen is referring to? Where might we look for evidence of this? Boisen is silent on this issue. In retrospect, his analysis of the inner conflict of the emotionally distressed, in spite of his many fresh insights, must be judged as simplistic. In a final essay on this subject, Boisen lamented the fact that his suggestions regarding Jesus' inner world were largely ignored by psychologists, theologians, and biblical scholars alike.[26] He was not aware of the degree to which his thinking was both ahead of its time and in need of fresh psychological input.

Psychoanalytic Perspectives

"Fresh psychological input" was already available when Boisen wrote, although for some reason he failed to utilize it. I refer to the epochal contributions of Sigmund Freud to our understanding of the genesis and development of human emotions. In trying now to summarize what these were, especially those that relate most directly to the subject at hand, it should first be recalled that they grew out of Freud's interest in understanding and helping people afflicted with neuroses—that is, persons whose contact with reality was by and large normal, but who nevertheless were emotionally disturbed to a degree that impaired their sexual and vocational capacities (their ability to "work and love," as Freud once put it).

Among the many insights that Freud eventually put forward in explanation of this condition (some tentative and now questionable), there was one that he himself singled out as possibly his most important contribution to the "science of man" (as he referred to it). This was the realization, which dawned on him early in his research, that the problems of people who suffer in this way are rooted in forgotten or "repressed" childhood experiences with parents, and more particularly in a poor resolution of what he termed "the central drama of the childhood years," the Oedipus Complex. Since it is Freud's insights into this emotional complex that have played the central role in the few psychohistorical probes into the life of Jesus that have appeared thus far (and do so as well in my own inquiry)—and since it is this facet of Freud's psychology that has stood up best under subsequent scientific scrutiny—it is important that something be said here, in a provisional way at least, about this aspect of the Freudian legacy in particular.[27]

What Freud meant by the Oedipus Complex is already hinted at by the name itself. Oedipus is the leading character in the Greek drama *Oedipus Rex*, which revolves about the fate of a young king who had unwittingly murdered his father and married his mother. Freud suggested that the enduring emotional impact of this play and others like it may be due to the fact that all of us in the course of our lives go through an Oedipus-like drama. Typically, in the years from three to seven a boy will form a close, sexually-charged bond with his mother (the parent of the opposite sex) and consequently find himself in competition with his father (the parent of the same sex). To become free from this bond with the mother and sexually mature, this romantic triangle must be resolved. This resolution happens usually through an emotionally-charged process during which the incestuous components of the maternal tie are weakened or dissolved because of the child's fear or respect for his father. As this process unfolds, the son typically identifies with the father and incorporates his values as superego or conscience, the core features of which, Freud wrote, are the repression or interdiction of incest (lust for the mother) and hate (of the father), emotions indigenous to the oedipal triangle.

In the case of male neurotics, however, Freud discovered that the emotional ties to the mother and hatred of the father are still strong (even if partially repressed), preventing those so afflicted from achieving adequate separation and autonomy from either parent and simultaneously inhibiting their capacity for heterosexual relations because of the depleted sense of male identity and the inhibiting incest taboo in force within the still too close tie to the mother. Furthermore, the failure of such men to achieve a solid identification with their fathers condemns them to an ongoing emotional tug-of-war with male authority figures generally ("ambivalence," Freud called it). In short, neurotic men are caught up in emotional conflicts that should have been resolved earlier in life but were not. Their hostile feelings toward "father-figures" and their often dependent, sexually-conflicted feelings toward "mother" figures are transference phenomena, unconscious replays of the still binding child-parent relationships.

Strangely, by mid-century almost no one had examined the psyche of Jesus from this point of view. This is all the more surprising when we recognize that Freud himself led the way, rather successfully, in illuminating the lives of certain "great men" by taking a second look at what could be learned about them through more careful attention to their developmental histories in the light of psychoanalysis.[28] Even today, with the amplification of the Freudian developmental outline in the work of Erik Erikson and Daniel Levinson and with the increasingly resourceful application of these insights to the lives of such world leaders as Luther, Gandhi, and others,[29] there is still virtually no serious discussion of the life of Jesus in this light.

Several somewhat fragmentary efforts along this line have come to my attention, however, and suggest, in my opinion, the lines along which further study of the psychology of Jesus must travel if it is going to achieve any significant results.

The first of these is a book-length study entitled *Some Aspects of the Life of Jesus from the Psychological and Psycho-analytic Point of View* (1923) by Georges Berguer, a Swiss academician.[30] Berguer argues that what stands out when we examine the life of Jesus in this light is Jesus' truly remarkable rapport with "the father." We see this initially in the story of his visit with his parents to the temple at twelve, when, after having been lost to them for three days and then found, he responded incredulously: "How is it that you sought me? Did you not know that I must be about my father's business?" (Luke 2:49). According to Berguer, this incident was the occasion when Jesus first became "aware of a difference between his own experience and that of his parents."[31] He now knew that he had a relationship with the Father they did not know of, and this inner consciousness never left him. It was confirmed and tested during his baptism and temptations and emerged as the moving force of his messianic mission. "In Jesus," Berguer believes, "*life with the Father* assumed a character of peaceful and normal reality such as is not to be found in any one else."[32] For this very reason, he concludes, Jesus ought to be regarded as standing at the forefront of human spiritual and moral evolution, because of the higher moral consciousness this exemplary resolution of the Oedipus Complex brings with it.[33]

A quite different picture of Jesus' inner world emerges in a second psychoanalytic foray into the life of Jesus: Jane Darroch's "An Interpretation of the Personality of Jesus" (1947).[34] In this study Jesus' reply to his parents in the incident at the temple at twelve, far from pointing to an exceptional rapport with the father (as Berguer suggested), is viewed as "characteristically adolescent." Jesus is "using his belief that he was the son of God to score over his real parents and adopt an attitude of moral superiority to them."[35] This repressed hostility toward his parents is also manifested in his harsh criticism of the Pharisees and his rather free attitude toward the law.[36] While ostensibly setting a high value on humility, subconsciously Jesus entertained "a phantasy of being a far better parent-figure than he unconsciously felt his parents to have been to him, one who would be loving and humble instead of unloving and proud."[37] Jesus' too high estimate of himself left him with a residue of repressed guilt, however, and this is the reason for his identification with sinners.[38] "The father of the prodigal son may represent the father whom Jesus, when a naughty child, had desired in vain."[39] Even his emphasis on love and forgiveness may have been "a reaction against the harsh and cruel aspect of his own personality, as well as against parents who were or seemed cruelly severe."[40] Two conceptions of God seem to have existed side by side in the mind of Jesus, Darroch speculates. One of them, less explicitly expressed, may have represented the terrifying father whom he actually felt to exist during his infancy; the other, the more explicitly expressed, represented the ideal father whom he wished to have and be to others. "That the desire for unresisting parents was unusually strong in the unconscious mind of Jesus is suggested by the various passages in which he exhorts to non-resistance against injury."[41] Darroch's picture of Jesus is thus of someone entangled in extremely ambivalent attitudes toward parents and authority figures generally, due to an unresolved Oedipus Complex—the opposite conclusion to that of Berguer.

The main theme of a third psychoanalytic study of Jesus, that of R. S. Lee, *Freud and Christianity* (1948), is more in line with that of Berguer. After a detailed exposition of Freudian theory, Lee asks what can be hypothesized in this light regarding Jesus' experience of his growing-up years. His answer is that "Christ showed no signs of mother-fixation but had completely resolved his Oedipus Complex, not merely as a child, but in his sublimist relations with God the Father."[42] Lee emphasizes that the consequence of this resolution was that Jesus not only succeeded in forming a healthy emotional identification with God as Father (superego religion), but did so in such a relaxed and confident manner that he was free for "reality testing" (ego religion). His God, therefore, was not only a divine sanction of morality, but the inner truth about the world (the fulfillment of Ego as well as Superego).

But how, more concretely, did Jesus arrive at such a novel resolution of his Oedipus Complex? Lee admits that the evidence regarding this question is sparse, but like both Darroch and Berguer, he points to the story of Jesus' visit to the temple at twelve as a possible source of some important clues. What catches his eye in this story, however, is not Jesus' reply to his parents but the fact that on this occasion he was observed "both hearing and asking questions" (Luke 2:46). This is evidence of an inquisitive mind at work. Jesus was "discovering an Ego-God, testing and reflecting over what he had learned, using insight to get an understanding of God and the world." His success in doing so, Lee argues, is reflected in his later parables where this same reality-oriented outlook is so magnificently demonstrated. In those too we see Jesus "drawing illustrations from a wide range of everyday things and events" and showing an interest "in every aspect of life."[43] Jesus obviously understood life and loved it, Lee concludes, and was not a dreamer of fantasies.

A final more recent (and more nuanced) attempt at sketching a psychoanalytically informed portrait of Jesus occurs in a provocative series of articles on "genius and neurosis" first published in two issues of the *Psychoanalytic Review* (1968) and then subsequently shortened and popularized for *Psychology Today*.[44] The author, Matthew Besdine, on the basis of clinical experience and detailed study of the personal histories of acknowledged geniuses, concluded that the lives of such persons are frequently characterized by an unresolved Oedipus Complex, fear of love, a strong homosexual element (either overt or latent), an underlying sense of guilt, great egocentricity, difficulty in relating consistently to the opposite sex, exorbitant striving for recognition, strong paranoid and masochistic trends, and significant narcissism. This, of course, is no more than a summary of the typical symptoms of neurosis as psychoanalysis has encountered them in case after case.

What is unique about Besdine's studies is his fresh, sharply focused investigation of an old problem: why is it that *geniuses* (men and women of extraordinary talent and achievement) so frequently suffer in this way? His answer focuses on the *mother* as the decisive factor in the genesis of both genius and neurosis.[45]

The neurotic genius, he writes, seems to develop in a family constellation dominated by a "strong affect-hungry mother" and an "absent, inept, distant, or aloof, or gentle father." The result is "obsessively dedicated mothering *by a single parent*." This he calls "*Jocasta* mothering," Jocasta being the mother of Oedipus in the Greek drama. The research indicates that "negligible mothering" produces retardation, "reluctant mothering" low achievers, "average mothering" average achievement, "dedicated mothering" (along with "dedicated fathering") high achievement without neurosis, and "Jocasta mothering" genius with neurosis.[46] By singling out her son for a special and exclusive relation extending well beyond the time when such a relation should normally dissolve in favor of the son's identification with his father, the Jocasta mother contributes to that preemptive grandiosity, emotional dependency, and sexual confusion that make it so difficult for him later on in life to marry and relate to others effectively. At the same time, however, through this same concentration of her attention and affection on this one special son, she evokes in him, when the necessary potential is there, an extraordinary development of talents and gifts, especially in the verbal and intellectual sphere. Thus the very same qualities of mothering that produce neurosis produce genius as well. Genius and neurosis occur so frequently in combination because they share the same originating matrix.

Besdine gives specific examples of men of genius who suffered in this way and on closer inspection, also turn out to have been mothered in this manner: Goethe, da Vinci, Michelangelo, Proust, Dostoevsky, and Freud. And in his *Psychology Today* article of January 1969, Besdine put forward the suggestion that the name of Jesus of Nazareth might legitimately be added to this list as well.

> Indeed, it could be argued that the life of the historical Nazarene, as we know it from the Gospels, bears the clear imprint of Jocasta-mothered genius. There is, for instance, the ineffectual, older father; the astonishing intellectual precocity; the final rejection of the mother; the absence of any sexual relations with women, yet the intense sympathy for the prostitute; the vanity, the egocentricity and fig-blasting temper; the exclusively male band of disciples and companions; the beautiful, profound, lovingly simple stories; the emphasis on childlikeness; the search for an all-loving all wise and powerful Father; the guilt, the atonement, the courting of and achievement of personal destruction, and finally, the staggering accomplishment: the creation of a complex picture or image, in which men for two thousand years have read the death of the body on the Cross or pin wheel of the world, and the entrance into a proper spiritual home through that necessary death.[47]

This is a provocative characterization, and coming as it does in the context of an illuminating discussion of the developmental dynamics of great men, it deserves our attention. If Besdine's description of Jesus is correct, however, then Lee's must be wrong and Berguer's one-sided. Far from making a successful passage through his Oedipus Complex, as Lee and Berguer would have it, Besdine's Jesus, like the Jesus of Darroch, would appear instead to be neurotic. But here too there are questions that immediately come to mind. What evidence is there, for example, that Jesus' father was either "old" or "ineffectual," as Besdine intimates? Furthermore, if Jesus was capable of a "final rejection of the mother," how does that correspond to his being a "Jocasta-mothered genius," where the bond with the mother is typically so intense that it is virtually impossible to terminate it? Using Besdine's own categories, could it not be suggested that Jesus' personality bears more the imprint of "dedicated mothering" (rather than "*Jocasta* mothering"), where the *father too* plays a significant role in the life of the child and the outcome generally is high achievement, but without neurosis?

The important point is, however, that with the studies by Berguer, Darroch, Lee, and Besdine, Jesus' psyche is at last being examined in developmental categories congruent with modern psychological research and the psychological outlook of our culture generally.[48]

Other Approaches

I am aware, of course, that in the last several decades the psychology pioneered by Freud and elaborated by "neo-Freudians" like Erikson, Besdine, and others has not gone unchallenged and that numerous schools of psychology have arisen professing to have discovered alternative ways of understanding and healing the emotional disorders. Freudian and neo-Freudian preoccupation with the Oedipus Complex especially has been a thorn of offense to many, and is the one element of a psychoanalytic-oriented psychology most often missing or severely modified among those who go a different way.[49]

I am also conscious of the fact that adherents and practitioners of these alternative schools have increasingly paid tribute to Jesus by analyzing him from their point of view. So, for example, Jay Haley (*The Power Tactics of Jesus Christ*, 1969), approaching the subject from an Adlerian perspective, musters evidence in support of his thesis that Jesus was an unusually cunning, power-hungry revolutionary bent on establishing a dictatorship over the Jewish establishment.[50] Raymond Lloyd, on the other hand, thinks that just the opposite was the case. In two wide-ranging articles entitled "Cross and Psychosis," in which he takes his psychological clues from Melanie Klein's analytic point of view, he suggests that Jesus was probably not power-hungry enough, so that when, in the course of his public ministry, he aroused the envy and hostility of others, it produced in him an emotional crisis, leading, at the time of his last visit to Jerusalem, to a manic-depressive psychosis.[51]

Others have assessed Jesus' psychology somewhat more positively. The Jungian psychiatrist Edward Edinger, for example, speaks of him as "the paradigm of the individuating ego," in a 1973 publication, *Ego and Archetype*.[52] And for Rosemary Haughton, an exponent of transactional analysis, he is perhaps the supreme example of a personality set free of "parent-scripts" and thereby uniquely able to foster freedom in others, "in a world populated by 'scripted' people."[53] Somewhat similarly, religious psychologist Donald Capps views Jesus as an example (due to his illegitimacy) of "an endangered self" who through the experience of being affirmed as "the true son of 'Abba' [God] and no other" became powerful in affirming other wounded selves.[54] Others have written of the striking compatibility between the way Jesus helped the people he met find meaning and the meaning-oriented therapy of Victor Frankl.[55] A New York City psychiatrist, O. Quentin Hyder, in still another study, acknowledges that Jesus' self-identity might indeed make him vulnerable to the charge of delusions of grandeur, but after reviewing four basic psychiatric categories in which such delusions may occur, he concludes that "Jesus' patterns of thought, speech, behavior, and interpersonal relationships were not those of known patterns in people who are mentally ill." On the contrary, he argues, Jesus is the very epitome of mental health and the exponent of teachings that are strikingly parallel to those that undergird modern psychotherapy.[56]

These studies are provocative but rather incomplete, and tend to be either wholly negative or wholly positive, giving the impression of one-sidedness. Furthermore, because they pay little or no attention to oedipal dynamics, the Gospel data having to do with Jesus' parental attitudes is either overlooked entirely or dealt with in a cursory way. I might add that in these studies too, no less than in most of the previous ones referred to in this survey, too little attention is paid to the established results of historical Jesus research. As a consequence, information reflective of the theology or piety of the early church is frequently used to interpret the Jesus of history.

Summary and Conclusions

Since the shift away from a disease-model of emotional illness and the advent since Freud of a psychogenic, developmental model, there has yet to appear a really thorough investigation of the psychology of Jesus in this light. And yet questions of a psychological nature keep recurring, and a steadily growing stream of studies attempting to say at least something about Jesus in this respect (either positively or negatively) testifies to the pressing need for a more intelligible "psychological model" in christology, as McIntyre once termed it.[57]

From the very beginning of the modern discussion, there seems to have been an intuition that the inner lives of "great men" like Jesus might one day be more fully appreciated were we to understand better the interconnections between their extraordinary achievements and the emotional stresses and strains confronting them. Indisputably Jesus at thirty was an exceptionally gifted person with an intense drive to accomplish something. Any approach to the psyche of Jesus that does not shed light on that fact or indicate how this links up with other known facets of his life is obviously deficient.

Besdine's identification of the role of a Jocasta-type mother in fostering both genius and disturbance is suggestive in this regard, but questions must be raised as to the degree to which Jesus actually does conform to the prototype Besdine outlines. Berguer and Lee, working with a similar psychodynamic model, differ with Besdine in their assessment of at least one crucial issue. There is ample evidence, they argue, that in Jesus' case the emotional tie to his mother was terminated and transcended through an especially meaningful identification with his father. And yet in making this point they have paid no attention at all to evidence cited by others pointing in quite other directions. Undeniably Jesus' familial relations at thirty were strained and his self-identity, however interpreted, appears to be extraordinary. Also his celibacy, if such it was, requires more than passing attention in the light of our current perceptions of the role of sexuality in emotional development.

The early Christian theologian who observed that Jesus was "tempted as we are" (Heb. 4:15) and "learned obedience through what he suffered" (Heb. 5:8) anticipated a fundamental principle of modern developmental psychology, stated well by Boisen when he wrote that "sanity" is not a static quality, not a given, but an achievement, a resolution of personal conflicts of various types and degrees of severity. Can the temptations and developmental conflicts specific to the historical Jesus be better understood? Were we able to do so—which is the aim of this inquiry—we might gain a deeper appreciation and understanding of the whole message of his life.

Notes

Preface

1. Roland Bainton, *Behold the Christ: A Portrayal in Words and Pictures* (New York: Harper & Row, 1974); Jaroslav Pelikan, *Jesus through the Centuries, His Place in the History of Culture* (New Haven: Yale University Press, 1985).

2. For a recent example, see N. T. Wright, *Jesus and the Victory of God* (Minneapolis: Fortress Press, 1996), who thinks the study of Jesus' psyche is "impossible" since "it is hard enough [for 'pastors, psychiatrists and psychotherapists'] to understand the inner workings of someone's psyche . . . when they co-operate with the process and answer one's questions" (p. 479). On the way historical Jesus studies inevitably focus on aspects of his personality, and in doing so make him vulnerable to psychological inquiry, see chapter 1 (also the essay in the Appendix on "The Psychological Study of Jesus," n. 1).

3. The historian Peter Gay, in a cogent defense of this approach, characterizes psychohistory "at its most ambitious" as an "orientation rather than a speciality," "a style of seeing the past" that can "inform" and "enrich" other approaches "without disturbing" them or being "reductionist" (*Freud for Historians* [New York: Oxford University Press, 1985], 210).

4. Albert Nolan, *Jesus before Christianity* (Maryknoll, N.Y.: Orbis Books, 1978), 117.

Chapter 1

1. John S. Dunne, *A Search for God in Time and Memory* (New York: Macmillan Paperback Edition, 1971), 13.

2. For an overview and critique of these studies, see the essay on this subject in the Appendix.

3. Further to this point, see under "Presuppositions."

4. For a useful summing up of the earlier results of historical Jesus research, see Leslie Mitton, *Jesus: The Fact behind the Faith* (Grand Rapids: Eerdmans, 1974). The impact of this research on contemporary thought is discussed in the works of Leander Keck, *A Future for the Historical Jesus: The Place of Jesus in Preaching and Theology* (Nashville and New York: Abingdon Press, 1971); Hans Küng, *On Being a Christian* (New York: Doubleday, 1976); Edward Schillebeeckx, *Jesus: An Experiment in Christology* (New York: Seabury Press, 1979); James M. Robinson, *A New Quest of the Historical Jesus* (Missoula: Scholars Press, 1979), among others. Scholarly developments in the quest since 1980 are traced and critiqued by Marcus J. Borg, *Jesus in Contemporary Scholarship* (Valley Forge: Trinity Press International, 1994); Ben Witherington III, *The Jesus Quest: The Third Search for the Jew of Nazareth* (Downers Grove: InterVarsity Press, 1995); Craig A. Evans, *Life of Jesus Research, An Annotated Bibliography*, rev. ed. (Leiden, New York, Cologne: E. J. Brill, 1996).

5. See especially the essays in *The Myth of God Incarnate*, ed. John Hick (London: SCM, 1977).

6. See especially his "Eight Ages of Man," in *Childhood and Society*, 2d ed. (New York: W. W. Norton, 1963), 247–74, and "Human Strength and the Cycle of Generations," in *Insight and Responsibility* (New York: W. W. Norton, 1964), 111–34. For a cogent analysis and appropriation of Erikson's work, see Don Browning, *Generative Man: Psychoanalytic Perspectives* (Philadelphia: Westminster, 1973); James Fowler, *Stages of Faith, The Psychology of Human Development and the Quest for Meaning* (San Francisco: Harper & Row, 1981).

7. Browning, *Generative Man*, pp. 12f., writes that "psychoanalysis has become the dominant symbolic in the Western world for the organization of the character of modern man." This fact is reflected in the mushrooming of psychohistorical research; regarding this, see William J. Gilmore, *Psychohistorical Inquiry: A Comprehensive Research Bibliography* (New York and London: Garland, 1984).

8. William Phipps, *Was Jesus Married?* (New York: Harper & Row, 1971); *The Sexuality of Jesus* (New York: Harper & Row, 1973).

9. Symptomatic of growing interest in Jesus' celibacy is Gerald Sloyan's attention to this subject in his popular summary of research on Jesus, *Jesus in Focus: A Life in Its Setting* (Mystic, Conn.: Twenty-third Publications, 1983), 129–32; see also Samuel Terrien's comments in his important work, *Till the Heart Sings: A Biblical Theology of Manhood and Womanhood* (Philadelphia: Fortress, 1985), 124–26. Earlier discussions of this issue are reviewed by John Hayes in *From Son of God to Super Star: Twentieth Century Interpretations of Jesus* (Nashville: Abingdon, 1976), 223–34.

10. E. P. Sanders, *Jesus and Judaism* (Philadelphia: Fortress Press, 1985), 271; Martin Hengel, *The Charismatic Leader and His Followers* (New York: Crossroad, 1981; first German edition, 1968), 64.

11. David Flusser, *Jesus* (New York: Herder and Herder, 1969), 22.

12. Schillebeeckx, *Jesus*, 270.

13. Gerald O'Collins, *What Are They Saying about Jesus?* (New York: Paulist Press, 1977), 15.

14. Note the way these questions begin to intrude into J. A. T. Robinson's *The Human Face of God* (London: SCM, 1973), 56–66.

15. On the interplay of philosophical dogma and psychology in the christological debates of the first three centuries, see Theodor Reik, *Dogma and Compulsion: Psychoanalytic Studies of Religion and Myth* (New York: International Universities Press, 1957), 24–161.

16. Regarding this issue as an important factor in the writing of our earliest Gospel, Mark, see Ralph Martin, *Mark, Evangelist and Theologian* (Grand Rapids: Zondervan, 1973), 214–19.

17. Regarding this "corrective" role of historical Jesus studies, see the comments of David Tracy in *Consensus in Theology? A Dialogue with Hans Küng and Edward Schillebeeckx*, ed. Leonard Swidler (Philadelphia: Westminster, 1980), 36–39.

18. For an informed discussion of these methods and criteria, see Schillebeeckx, *Jesus*, 81–100; M. Eugene Boring, "Criteria of Authenticity: The Lucan Beatitudes as a Test Case," *Forum* 1/4 (December 1985): 3–38.

19. After a careful review of the criteria of authenticity proposed by recent scholars, Graham Stanton (*The Gospels and Jesus* [Oxford University Press, 1989], 163), states that "we have no option but to conclude that in most cases certainty eludes us. On the other hand there is little evidence which suggests that large numbers of traditions were simply made up by Christians in the post-Easter period. And there are good grounds for accepting that on the whole oral traditions were preserved carefully, though they certainly were reinterpreted in order to make them relevant in differing settings."

20. The following studies have proven to be especially seminal for this particular inquiry: David Flusser, *Jesus*; Joachim Jeremias, *New Testament Theology*, pt. 1, *The Proclamation of Jesus* (London: SCM, 1971); Geza Vermes, *Jesus the Jew: A Historian's Reading of the Gospels* (Philadelphia: Fortress Press, 1973); James Dunn, *Jesus and the Spirit* (London: SCM, 1975); Ben Meyer, *The Aims of Jesus* (London: SCM, 1979); Martin Hengel, *The Charismatic Leader*; J. Ramsey Michaels, *Servant and Son: Jesus in Parable and Gospel* (Atlanta: John Knox, 1981); Marcus Borg, *Conflict, Holiness and Politics in the Teaching of Jesus* (Lewistown, N.Y.: Edwin Mellen, 1984); John P. Meier, *A Marginal Jew, Rethinking the Historical Jesus*, vol. 1, *The Roots of the Problem and the Person* (Doubleday: New York, 1991); and vol. 2, *Mentor, Message, and Miracles* (Doubleday: New York, 1994).

21. For a comprehensive review of the research bearing upon psychoanalytic theory, much of it supportive of its perspectives, see Seymour Fisher and Roger Greenberg, *The Scientific Credibility of Freud's Theories and Therapy* (New York: Basic Books, 1977); regarding the empirical foundations of Erikson's life-stage theories, see Fowler, *Stages of Faith*, 106. In his bibliographical review

William Gilmore, *Psychohistorical Inquiry*, cites over 4,000 books, book chapters, articles, dissertations, and papers devoted to this subject.

22. For an overview of Freud's legacy in this regard and its relevance for Jesus studies, see the discussion of "Psychoanalytic Perspectives" in the Appendix; for an account of Erikson's and Levinson's studies as they bear upon Jesus' "Age Thirty Transition," see chapter 8.

Chapter 2

1. David Flusser, *Jesus* (New York: Herder and Herder, 1969), 20.

2. Sigmund Freud, *Leonardo da Vinci and a Memory of His Childhood* (New York: W. W. Norton, 1964), 32.

3. Erik Erikson, *Young Man Luther: A Study in Psychoanalysis and History* (New York: W. W. Norton, 1958), 23.

4. For a review of the issues involved in translating this text, see especially *Mary in the New Testament*, ed. Raymond Brown, Karl Donfried, Joseph Fitzmyer, and John Reumann (Philadelphia: Fortress Press; New York/Ramsey/Toronto: Paulist Press, 1978), 51–58. An attempt by Dom Henry Wansbrough, "Mark III.21—Was Jesus Out of His Mind?" *New Testament Studies* 58 (1971–72): 233–35, to translate this passage as though it were "the crowd" that is "beside itself" and Jesus' "followers" rather than his "family" who misunderstood him, is refuted by J. D. Crossan, "Mark and the Relatives of Jesus," *Novum Testamentum* 15 (1973): 81–113, and David Wenham, "The Meaning of Mark III.21," *New Testament Studies* 21 (1974–75): 295–300.

5. Günther Bornkamm, *Jesus of Nazareth* (New York: Harper and Brothers, 1960); C. H. Dodd, *The Founder of Christianity* (New York: Macmillan, 1970); Etienne Trocmé, *Jesus as Seen by His Contemporaries* (Philadelphia: Westminster, 1973); Joseph Klausner, *Jesus of Nazareth: His Life, Times and Teaching* (New York: Macmillan, 1926), 280; David Flusser, *Jesus* (New York: Herder and Herder, 1969), 20-21; Geza Vermes, *Jesus the Jew* (Philadelphia: Fortress Press, 1981), 33–34.

6. Vincent Taylor, *The Gospel according to St. Mark* (New York: Macmillan, 1952), 235. Vermes, *Jesus the Jew*, comments that "the scandalous incongruity of this statement is the best guarantee of its historicity" (p. 33). See also Martin Hengel, *The Charismatic Leader and His Followers* (New York: Crossroad), 64; G. D. Kilpatrick, "Jesus, His Family and His Disciples," in *The Historical Jesus: A Sheffield Reader*, ed. Craig A. Evans and Stanley E. Porter, (Sheffield: Sheffield Academic Press, 1995), 13–28; reprinted from *Journal for the Study of the New Testament* 15 (1982): 3–19.

7. Klausner, *Jesus of Nazareth*, 280.

8. On the basis of papyri evidence (where ages are often given in multiples of five) Henry J. Cadbury, "Some Lukan Expressions of Time (Lexical Notes on Luke-Acts VII)," *Journal of Biblical Literature* 82 (1963): 275f., suggests that

Luke's "about thirty" was meant to convey that Jesus was between twenty-five and thirty-five at this time.

9. Hengel, *The Charismatic Leader*, regards this highly negative reaction of Jesus' family to his mission as not only historical but as proof that the traditional picture of Jesus as "Rabbi" is incorrect: "Had Jesus been a rabbi learned in the Torah or a teacher of wisdom like Ben Sira he would doubtless have met with a more positive reception, and with someone of that sort the closest members of his family would hardly have set out to fetch him back home" (p. 65).

10. The historicity of this saying is particularly emphasized by Martin Hengel, *The Charismatic Leader*: "There is hardly one logion of Jesus which more sharply runs counter to law, piety and custom [of that time]" (p. 14).

11. Jacques Maritain, *On the Humanity and Grace of Jesus* (New York: Herder and Herder, 1969), 128.

12. Regarding these tensions and this gulf, see Louis Berguer's comments in his pioneering work, *Aspects of the Life of Jesus from the Psychological and Psychoanalytic Point of View* (New York: Harcourt Brace and Co., 1923), 102; also G. D. Kilpatrick, "Jesus, His Family and His Disciples." i

Chapter 3

1. Donald P. Gray, "Was Jesus a Convert?" *Religion in Life* 43 (Winter 1974): 454.

2. According to Mark and Luke this "voice from heaven" spoke directly *to* Jesus ("*Thou* art my beloved Son . . ."), whereas in Matthew 3:17 it addressed the bystanders ("*This* is my beloved Son . . ."). Thus Matthew's version changed what was undoubtedly a private experience into a public event. John's Gospel does the same by interpreting the descent of the Spirit-dove (in reliance on Luke 3:22) as a literal sign meant for John the Baptist (John 1:32).

3. Joachim Jeremias, *New Testament Theology*, pt. 1, *The Proclamation of Jesus* (London: SCM, 1971), 45.

4. Ibid., 51–56; James Dunn, *Jesus and the Spirit* (London: SCM, 1975), 62–65; J. Ramsey Michaels, *Servant and Son: Jesus in Parable and Gospel* (Atlanta: John Knox, 1981), 36–39.

5. Dunn, *Jesus and the Spirit*, 63. Michaels, *Servant and Son*, suggests that any hesitation about acknowledging that Jesus might have had the experience attributed to him in these texts "may be traceable more to a stubborn expectation that Jesus must be unique than to a sober assessment of the evidence. Some would rather believe that the church attributed this experience to him falsely, than run the risk of placing him in such a problematic category as that of a visionary or seer. And yet if we are simply describing the phenomenon, a visionary is exactly what Jesus was" (p. 37). Flusser, *Jesus*, also states that "nothing that we have learned casts any doubt upon the historicity of Jesus' experience at his baptism in the Jordan" (p. 29).

6. Regarding Jesus' prophetic consciousness, see Jeremias, *N.T. Theology*, 76–80.

7. Ibid., 59.

8. Ibid., 56.

9. Dunn, *Jesus and the Spirit*, 65. This is also the conclusion drawn by Marcus J. Borg in *Jesus: A New Vision, Spirit, Culture, and the Life of Discipleship* (San Francisco: Harper & Row, 1987). Borg writes that "this vision is reminiscent of the 'call narratives' of the prophets. Like them, his [Jesus'] ministry began with an intense experience of the Spirit of God" (p. 42).

10. Ibid., 66.

11. The conclusion of Jeremias, *N. T. Theology*, p. 258, that "'Son of God' is completely unknown as a messianic title in Palestinian Judaism" may need to be qualified slightly in the light of the recent publication of a text from Qumran (4Q246) in which "Son of God" is used to refer to an apocalyptic figure who is worshiped by the nations following an end-time battle, much like the Enochic "son of man" in 4 Ezra 13, although even here there is no explicit reference to this being the Messiah. Regarding this text and its messianic overtones, see John J. Collins, "The *son of god* Text from Qumran," *Journal for the Study of the New Testament*, Supplement Series, 84 (Sheffield: JSOT Press, 1993): 65–82. On the reluctance to use "Son of God" terminology for the Messiah in this period, see also Geza Vermes, *Jesus the Jew: A Historian's Reading of the Gospels* (New York: Macmillan, 1973), 197–99, and William Manson, *Jesus the Messiah* (London: Hodder and Stoughton, 1943), 105–9. Manson believes that the avoidance of this terminology was a reaction against "a manner of speech which savoured of mythology" (p. 106).

12. Regarding the debate over whether the words here refer exclusively to Isaiah 42:1 or to Psalm 2:7, see Dunn, *Jesus and the Spirit*, 62–67, 366, n. 73; 378, n. 122. Michaels, *Servant and Son*, 39–41, suggests that neither text is germane and that an alternative approach to their understanding must be sought.

13. Regarding this, see especially the chapter on "Jesus and Charismatic Judaism" in Vermes, *Jesus the Jew*, 58–82; and Jacob Neusner, *The Rabbinic Traditions about the Pharisees before 70*, pt. 1 (Leiden: E. J. Brill, 1971), 176–82.

14. Vermes, *Jesus the Jew*, 70.

15. Dunn, *Jesus and the Spirit*, 38, 40. The same point is stressed by Manson, *Jesus the Messiah*, 109.

16. Dunn, *Jesus and the Spirit*, 38.

17. Concerning Jesus' estimate of John, and their relationship, see Jeremias, *N.T. Theology*, 43–49; also Paul Hollenbach, "The Conversion of Jesus: From Jesus the Baptizer to Jesus the Healer," in *Aufstieg und Niedergang der Römischen Welt: Geschichte und Kultur Roms im Spiegel der neuen Forschung*, ed. Hildegard Temporini and Wolfgang Haase (Berlin and New York: Walter de Gruyter, 1982), 196–219.

18. Ben Meyer, *The Aims of Jesus* (London: SCM, 1979), 120. Michaels adds that by insisting that all "*needed* the forgiveness that his baptism represented"

John thereby reduced the most religious "'son of Abraham' to the level of a mere outsider submitting to a ritual of initiation into Israel" (*Servant and Son*, 23).

19. For the distinction between "sinners" and "people of the land" (*'am ha-aretz*), see E. P. Sanders, *Jesus and Judaism* (Philadelphia: Fortress Press, 1985), 174–211, and chap. 9, n. 16. Martin Hengel, *The Charismatic Leader and His Followers* (New York: Crossroad, 1981), 50, calls the "gap" between the scribal elite and these Torah-lax masses a distinguishing mark of the Palestinian Judaism of Jesus' day.

20. Matthew's account of this episode would imply that John the Baptist knew Jesus before his baptism, but in John's Gospel the Baptist twice declares that this was not the case: "I myself did not know him" (John 1:31, 33). Both here and again in Matt. 10:16f. Matthew edits the tradition to remove any suggestion of consciousness of sin on Jesus' part.

21. Vincent Taylor, *The Life and Ministry of Jesus* (London: Macmillan, 1961), 49.

22. For an alternative position, see John P. Meier, *A Marginal Jew: Rethinking the Historical Jesus*, vol. 2, *Mentor, Message, and Miracles* (New York: Doubleday, 1994), 112–16. Meier believes that "the mere fact of Jesus' acceptance of John's message and baptism does not yield sufficient data to form a judgment in the matter [of whether he was seeking forgiveness for himself]," since "confession of sins" in ancient Israel typically involved "a recounting of the infidelities and apostasies of Israel from early on down to one's own day" and not "a narcissistic reflection on self" (p. 113). The implication that communal confession of (Israel's) sins was what John the Baptist was calling for is not consistent with the personalized nature of his mission (see Luke 3:7-14); nor was this the focus of the mission of Jesus (see chap. 8 of the present work).

23. William James, *The Varieties of Religious Experience: A Study in Human Nature* (New York: Longmans, Green & Co., 1902; repr. ed., London: Collier-Macmillan, 1961), 78–113.

24. Pitrim Sorokin, *The Ways and Power of Love* (Chicago: Henry Regnery Co., 1967), 147.

25. James, *Varieties*, 114–42.

26. Walter Houston Clark, *The Psychology of Religion: An Introduction to Religious Experience and Behavior* (New York: Macmillan, 1958), characterizes conversion experiences of this type as following three well-defined stages: a period of unrest, a moment of illumination, followed by a time of inner harmony and spiritual vitality (pp. 193–95). On the process of conversion seen from a psychoanalytic point of view, see Geoffrey Paterson, "Regression in Healing and Salvation," *Pastoral Psychology* 19 (September 1968): 33–39.

27. For a similar conclusion see Donald Gray, "Was Jesus a Convert?" *Religion in Life* 43 (Winter 1974): 445–55. For a summary of the research on conversion, see V. Bailey Gillespie, *Religious Conversion and Personal Identity: How and Why People Change* (Birmingham: Religious Education Press, 1979).

28. A. J. Krailsheimer, *Conversion* (London: SCM, 1980), states that a pre-

dominant feature of the lives of the twelve religious leaders reviewed in his study (each of whom experienced a dramatic conversion) "is the marked tension or imbalance in family relationships" that existed prior to their conversions (p. 154).

Chapter 4

1. Erik Erikson, *Young Man Luther* (New York: W. W. Norton, 1958), 124.

2. For a survey of the historical improbabilities and contradictions between and within these two narratives, see John P. Meier, *A Marginal Jew: Rethinking the Historical Jesus*, vol. 1, *The Problem and the Person* (New York: Doubleday, 1991), 208–13. Meier concludes that "both narratives seem to be largely products of early Christian reflection on the salvific meaning of Jesus Christ in the light of OT prophecies" (p. 213).

3. The genealogies in Matthew 1:1-16 and Luke 3:23-38 presuppose paternity through Joseph and thus appear to be older than the virgin birth traditions, or at least to come from communities in which it was taken for granted that Joseph was Jesus' father and a descendent of David. Since Jesus did not object to being called "David's son" (Matt. 20:29-32//Mark 10:46-52//Luke 18:35-43), it may be that the Davidic descent of his family was common knowledge (see Rom. 1:3; also our comments in chap. 8, n. 55). The editorial insertion of "as was supposed" in Luke 3:23 ("being the son, as was supposed, of Joseph . . .") was thus needed to harmonize Luke's genealogy with his prior account of the virgin birth. In Matthew the same difficulty was dealt with through an editorial manipulation at the end (Matt. 1:16), where "Jacob" (Jesus' grandfather) is said to be "father of Joseph," but Joseph is not said to be "father of Jesus" (as the genealogy would lead us to expect), but "husband of Mary, of whom Jesus was born. . . ." Further to this issue, see Charles Guignebert, *Jesus* (New York: University Books, 1956), 115–16; Geza Vermes, *Jesus the Jew, A Historian's Reading of the Gospels* (New York: Macmillan, 1973), 215–17. Questions regarding Jesus' possible "illegitimacy" are discussed below (see n. 37).

4. Joseph Klausner, *Jesus of Nazareth: His Life, Times and Teaching* (New York: Macmillan, 1926), 238.

5. The best example is the second-century "Infancy Gospel of Thomas," translated by E. Hennecke, *New Testament Apocrypha* I, ed. W. Schneemelcher (London: SCM, 1963), 392–401.

6. This is Raymond Brown's conclusion in *The Birth of the Messiah* (Garden City, N.Y.: Doubleday, 1977) 526.

7. The notion that Jesus' siblings were children of Joseph by a previous marriage (the so-called "Epiphanian solution") is refuted by Meier, *Marginal Jew*, vol. 1, who traces its roots to the presentation of Joseph in the *Protevangelium Jacobi*, "a wildly imaginative folk narrative that is outrageously inaccurate about things Jewish" (p. 324).

8. The exceptional status, rights, and role of the first-born son in biblical culture are succinctly summarized in the essay by J. Milgrom, *Interpreter's Dic-*

tionary of the Bible, Supplementary Volume (Nashville: Abingdon, 1976), 337–38.

9. I will have more to say below about the way this and other sayings and stories of Jesus may reflect his own emotional experience and identity.

10. In the Greek Bible, Joshua, Jehoshua, and Jeshuah are all rendered by Jesus. On the popularity of this name during the time of Jesus and the significance of names generally in that culture, see Charles Guignebert *Jesus*, (New York: University Books, 1956), 76–78.

11. Eusebius, *The History of the Church from Christ to Constantine*, translated by G. A. Williamson (Minneapolis: Augsburg, 1965), 2.23.

12. For a graphic picture of this city as it existed in the time of Jesus (the result of recent archaeological excavations), see Richard A. Batey, *Jesus and the Forgotten City: New Light on Sepphoris and the Urban World of Jesus* (Grand Rapids: Baker Book House, 1991).

13. Vermes, *Jesus the Jew*, characterizes upper and lower Galilee as "a little island in the midst of unfriendly seas" (p. 44). Even the Judaism that came to expression there was highly suspect to the religious elite elsewhere, as the pejorative use of "Galilee" and "Galilean" in the Gospels themselves would suggest (John 7:41, 52).

14. George Wesley Buchanan, "Jesus and the Upper Classes," *Novum Testamentum* 7 (1964–65): 195–209. Buchanan notes that *tekton* (Mark 6:3), usually translated "carpenter," could also mean "contractor" and that Jesus' parables occasionally refer to the construction of larger buildings (Matt. 7:24-27//Luke 6:47-49 and Luke 14:28-30), not to carpentry as such. Indeed, from Paul's allusion to Jesus having once been rich (2 Cor. 8:9), Buchanan draws the conclusion that Jesus may have been relatively well-to-do during his pre-mission years and very much at home among the business elite of his world (tax-collectors and the like).

15. David Flusser, *Jesus* (New York: Herder and Herder, 1969), 20. For an alternative view, see John Dominic Crossan, *Jesus, A Revolutionary Biography* (San Francisco: HarperSanFrancisco, 1995), 25, who imagines Jesus as almost at the bottom of the social scale and illiterate ("since between 95 and 97 percent of the Jewish state was illiterate at the time"). For contradictory evidence pointing to a vigorous culture of reading and learning among pious Jews of this period, see Meier, *Marginal Jew*, vol. 1, 274–78.

16. William E. Phipps, *Was Jesus Married?* (New York: Harper & Row, 1971); *The Sexuality of Jesus* (New York: Harper & Row, 1973); see also Schalom Ben-Chorin, *Bruder Jesus* (Munich: List Verlag, 1967), 127–29.

17. Meier, *Marginal Jew*, vol. 1, notes that this explanation of Jesus' father's absence in the Gospel accounts of Jesus' mission (that he had died before that time) was the "traditional solution, already known in the patristic period," and that this is still "the most likely" one (p. 317).

18. Flusser, *Jesus*, is thus hardly correct when he writes that Jesus might have been "still quite a child" when his father died (p. 17).

19. This is Brown's conclusion in *Birth of the Messiah*, 540; also Meier, *Marginal Jew*, vol. 1, 225–27.

20. C. Milo Connick, *Jesus: The Man, the Mission, and the Message*, 2d ed. (Englewood, N.J.: Prentice-Hall, 1974), 131. William Barclay, *The Mind of Jesus* (London: SCM, 1960), 20, and Robert H. Stein, *Jesus the Messiah: A Survey of the Life of Christ* (Downers Grove: InterVarsity Press, 1966), 85, paint a similar picture. The "only thing we really know," writes Stein, "is that with the death of Joseph the responsibilities of caring for the mother and family fell on the oldest son—Jesus. . . . Thus for the period after Joseph's death to the time of his ministry, Jesus was the active breadwinner and responsible head of the family" (p. 85).

21. For reviews of this frequently discussed topic, see, among others, Joachim Jeremias, *The Prayers of Jesus* (Philadelphia: Fortress Press, 1978), 75–79; Edward Schillebeeckx, *Jesus: An Experiment in Christology* (New York: Seabury, 1979), 256–71; Geza Vermes, *Jesus and the World of Judaism* (Philadelphia: Fortress Press, 1983), 39–43.

22. Jeremias, *Prayers of Jesus*, 11–65; also, James Dunn, *Christology in the Making* (London: SCM, 1980), 26–28. The Aramaic vocative, *Abba*, is preserved only once in Mark 14:36, but is generally thought to lie behind the short invocation "Father" (Greek: *pater*), which is so recurrent in Jesus' prayers.

23. For a comparison of God as father in the Bible with divine father figures in several contemporary ancient Near Eastern mythologies, see John W. Miller, *Biblical Faith and Fathering* (New York: Paulist Press, 1989), 43–54.

24. Vermes, *Jesus and the World of Judaism*, finds it quite striking and unusual that despite the many references to God's kingdom in the Gospels, Jesus "nowhere alludes to, or addresses, God as King, a fact all the more remarkable in that, together with its synonym 'Lord', *adonai*, 'King' occurs frequently in ancient Jewish prayer and continues to do so to this day." By contrast, Vermes observes, leaving aside Matthew 11:25//Luke 10:21 (which he does not attribute to Jesus), "in all but one of his other recorded prayers, and in his habitual speech, he uses 'Father'" (p. 39).

25. Jeremias, *N.T. Theology*, 67.

26. Ibid., 36. The way this word did in fact become sacred in this sense even among Jesus' Greek-speaking followers in the early church is indicated by its use not only in the congregations that Paul founded (Gal. 4:6) but in the far-flung churches of Rome (Rom. 8:15), where the cry "Abba" (uttered in the Spirit) was recognized as an authentic sign that one had become a child of God and a Christian.

27. Ibid., 61.

28. According to Jeremias, ibid., the meaning of this much debated sentence is: "only father and son really know each other" (p. 58).

29. In his perceptive treatment of this text, Hans-Ruedi Weber, *Jesus and the Children* (Geneva: World Council of Churches, 1979), 17–20, refers to this as a prophetic "symbolic action."

30. This is one of Jesus' "truly" sayings, where he uses the Hebrew "Amen" at the forefront of his statement (instead of at the end) to give it an added solemni-

ty. For further details on this usage, see Jeremias, *N.T. Theology*, 35f.

31. Ibid., 156.

32. For a review of what can be learned about Jesus' personal manner through the study of his parables, see John W. Miller, "Jesus' Personality as Reflected in His Parables," in *The New Way of Jesus*, ed. William Klassen (Newton, Kans.: Faith and Life, 1980), 56–72.

33. By contrast the role of women in his parables is rather limited. Regarding this, see the discussion of "Jesus and his mother" in chapter 5.

34. For details on this issue, see Jeremias, *N.T. Theology*, 210.

35. Edward Edinger, *Ego and Archetype* (New York: Putnam, 1972), 132. For a similar intuition, see Donald Capps, "The Desire to Be Another Man's Son: The Child Jesus," in *The Endangered Self*, Monograph Series, no. 2, ed. Richard K. Fenn and Donald Capps (Center for Religion, Self and Society, Princeton Theological Seminary, 1992), 21–36.

36. Edinger, *Ego and Archetype*, 132.

37. Arguments for illegitimacy put forward by Jane Schaberg, *The Illegitimacy of Jesus. A Feminist Theological Interpretation of the Infancy Narratives* (San Francisco: Harper & Row, 1987), are reviewed by Meier, *Marginal Jew*, vol. 1, 222–30, who writes that he can find no clearly attested tradition that Jesus was illegitimate "until close to the middle of the 2d century A.D." and then, as "a mocking, polemical reaction to the claims of the [Matthean and Lukan] Infancy Narratives, perhaps as filtered through popular disputes" (p. 230). Two New Testament texts sometimes cited as alluding to Jesus' illegitimacy, Mark 6:3 and John 8:41, are of doubtful relevance. The first, where Jesus is spoken of during a visit to Nazareth as "son of Mary" instead of "son of Joseph" (Mark 6:3), is hardly germane, since there is no evidence that referring to someone as son of the mother instead of the father is indicative of illegitimacy (see Meier, ibid., 226). In John 8:41, "Jews" who are described as seeking to kill Jesus are portrayed as defending their legitimacy as children of Abraham and of God against the charge of being fathered by "the devil" (John 8:44). The countercharge made against Jesus is that he is "a Samaritan" and has "a demon" (John 8:48), not that he is biologically illegitimate.

38. See n. 3 above.

39. Even Schaberg, *Illegitimacy of Jesus*, after an elaborate argument against Joseph's biological paternity goes on to state that he "accepted the child [Jesus] into his family" in "defiance of social expectations" (p. 153).

40. R. S. Lee, *Freud and Christianity* (Harmondsworth: Penguin, 1948), 109. For a brief description of the emotional challenges of the Oedipus Complex and their importance for adult emotionality, see "Psychoanalytic Perspectives" in the Appendix and the section on "Mothers and Sons" in chapter 5.

41. As noted in the Appendix, Georges Berguer, a Swiss academician who wrote one of the very first studies of this kind (*Some Aspects of the Life of Jesus from the Psychological and Psycho-analytic Point of View* [New York: Harcourt, Brace and Company, 1923], came to similar conclusions.

42. For the citations of Besdine's several essays on this subject, see the Appendix, n. 44.

43. Matthew Besdine, "Mrs. Oedipus," *Psychology Today* 2 (January 1969): 67. For a fuller citation and description of Besdine's portrait, see the Appendix.

44. J. Middleton Murry, *Jesus: Man of Genius* (New York: Harper & Brothers, 1926), 6.

Chapter 5

1. Joseph Klausner, *Jesus of Nazareth* (New York: Macmillan, 1926), 235.

2. For an analysis of these sources and the point of view of the earliest traditions, see especially *Mary in the New Testament*, ed. Brown, Donfried, Fitzmyer, and Reumann (Philadelphia: Fortress Press; New York/Ramsey/Toronto: Paulist Press, 1978); also Marina Warner, *Alone of All Her Sex: The Myth and the Cult of the Virgin Mary* (London: Quartet Books, 1976), 3–24.

3. The historicity of these unique Johannine traditions cannot, of course, be taken for granted; regarding this issue see Raymond Brown, *The Gospel According to John* (I–XII), The Anchor Bible 29 (New York: Doubleday, 1966), xlvii–li.

4. Ibid., 99.

5. Regarding the various meanings of this expression, see ibid., 99.

6. Gerald O'Collins in *What Are They Saying about Jesus?* (New York: Paulist Press, 1977), 68, has also noted this silence about mothers in Jesus' teachings and speculates that the reason might be either Jesus' "utterly untroubled relationship to his own mother," or a reserve regarding such language in rabbinic tradition. Since mothers play prominent roles in Hebrew scripture and maternal language can be used there even of God (Ps. 131:2; Isa. 66:13), this latter point seems weak. It is also unclear why an "utterly untroubled" maternal relationship would *inhibit* use of maternal language. The opposite seems more likely: a troubled relationship might well have this effect.

7. Antoine Vergote and Alvaro Tamayo, *The Parental Figures and the Representation of God: A Psychological and Cross-Cultural Study*, Religion and Society 21 (The Hague, Paris, New York: Mouton Publishers, 1981), 186. For a review of the research, see Rudolf Schaffer, *Mothering* (Cambridge: Harvard University Press, 1977).

8. On the importance of the mother's contribution to a child's developing relation with the father already in the first two years, see Richard Atkins, "Discovering Daddy: The Mother's Role," in *Father and Child: Developmental and Clinical Perspectives*, ed. S. Cath et al. (Boston: Little, Brown and Company, 1982), 139–49.

9. For a fuller account of the parental dynamics involved in these important childhood developments and their impact on adult emotionality, see the section "Psychoanalytic Perspectives" in the Appendix to this volume.

10. The importance of this "letting go" on the mother's part and of a son's

forming a bond of respect toward his father is highlighted by Vergote's research on parental images among schizophrenics, where "judge" appeared as a predominant factor in the mother-image and aspects of "law" and "authority" were missing in their perception of the father (*The Parental Figures*, 162–68).

11. On the subject of Jesus as an autonomous, faith-evoking figure, see especially the discussions in Leander Keck, *A Future for the Historical Jesus* (Grand Rapids: Eerdmans, 1977). 177–92; James Mackey, *Jesus the Man and the Myth, A Contemporary Christology* (New York/Ramsey: Paulist Press, 1979), 159–72; James Breech, *The Silence of Jesus: The Authentic Voice of the Historical Man* (Philadelphia: Fortress Press, 1983); and Erik Erikson, "The Galilee Sayings and the Sense of 'I'," *The Yale Review* 70 (Spring 1981): 321–62. Keck summarizes: "Jesus' whole career has to do with the trustworthiness of God and with the trusting response of man" (p. 183).

12. Psychoanalysts Françoise Dolto and Gérard Sévérin, *The Jesus of Psychoanalysis, Freudian Interpretation of the Gospel* (Garden City, N.Y.: Doubleday, 1979), 55–62, have captured some of the complexities involved in the relationship of a mother with an adult son urgently needing autonomy, in their comments on the interactions of Jesus and his mother as described in the story in John 2:1-11 of the marriage feast in Cana.

13. Parental loss as a factor in "genius" has been carefully researched by J. Marvin Eisenstadt, "Parental Loss and Genius," *American Psychologist* 33 (March 1978): 211–23. His study of 573 "eminent individuals" revealed that parental loss among this group was at a significantly earlier age than among the general population. Surprisingly, however, the statistics for this group were similar to the age of parental loss among psychotic, severely depressed, or suicidal patients. His explanation is that a child faced by the loss of one or both parents is suddenly compelled to master a new environment. For some this challenge may prove to be overwhelming, leading to mental and emotional breakdown. But others who begin life with an inborn potential for exceptional creativity are able to respond by going through what Eisenstadt calls a process of "creative mourning" and "overcompensation." The potential genius, he writes, translates this struggle for mastery, following the death of a parent, into a personal development that leads to a high degree of competency and superiority in an occupational field.

14. Regarding the special developmental problems of first-born sons see Hilda S. Rollman-Branch, "The First Born Child, Male: Vicissitudes of Preoedipal Problems," *International Journal of Psycho-Analysis* 47 (1966): 404–15. Using material from clinical practice and biographical data on acknowledged geniuses, she argues "that for the first-born, male, the resolution of the pre-oedipal ambivalence toward the mother is particularly problematical. He has been the privileged only child until he is displaced and then has no older sibling to serve as an auxiliary object. . . . Under unfavourable circumstances, both the first-born's ability to work and to love *may be* seriously impaired. Under favourable conditions, his creativity *may be* enhanced and his love relations with

women satisfactory" (p. 414). She notes that already Freud wrote "that if a man has been his mother's undisputed darling he retains throughout life the triumphant feeling, the confidence in success, which not seldom brings actual success along with it" (p. 404, quoted from Freud's essay, "A Childhood Recollection" from *Dichtung und Wahrheit*).

15. William Lamers, Jr., "The Absent Father," in *Fathering: Fact or Fable?* ed. Edward Stein (Nashville: Abingdon, 1977), 75–78, cites the following "common reactions" to the departure of a father from the home (whether through death or divorce): (1) rageful protests over desertion; (2) denial of loss and maintenance of an intense relationship with the lost parent; (3) persistent efforts at reunion and restitution; (4) arousal of irrational guilt and need for punishment; (5) exaggerated separation anxieties and fears of abandonment; (6) splitting of ambivalence toward the lost parent with a redirection of the hostility toward self or another; (7) a strong sense of narcissistic injury; (8) decrease of ego control following loss of ego and superego support; (9) precipitation of a wide variety of ego-repressive symptoms.

16. In one instance a son whose father was killed in a farming accident when he was an adolescent told me that the dilemma he felt over how long to remain at home was only resolved when his mother remarried. He was already twenty-five at the time, but "it was as though a burden had been lifted from my shoulders," he said. It was this that released him soon thereafter also to marry and establish a home of his own.

17. The significance of this transition to his public mission having occurred in or about Jesus' thirtieth year will be a focus of our discussion in chapter 8.

18. In relating Jesus' experience of God as "father" to his human experience of "father" I do not mean to imply that the one was simply a reflection or projection of the other. Nevertheless, the two do intersect—it could hardly be otherwise since these experiences, whatever their ultimate significance, happen to us and within us. John McDargh, *Psychoanalytic Object Relations Theory and the Study of Religion: On Faith and the Imaging of God* (Lanham: University Press of America, 1983), 118, distinguishes (with William James) between "nearer" and "further" sides of our sense of the reality of God and suggests that the one (the "further" side) is the "purview of theology proper," while the other (the "nearer" side of our experience of God as "something there") admits "of at least some psychological account."

Chapter 6

1. Vernon S. McCasland, *The Pioneer of Our Faith: A New Life of Jesus* (New York: McGraw-Hill, 1966), 31.

2. Regarding this phenomenon, see William Kelly, "Refathering in Counseling and Psychotherapy," in *Fathering: Fact or Fable?* ed. Edward Stein (Nashville: Abingdon, 1977), 108–38.

3. For a helpful discussion of this process, see Geoffrey Peterson, "Regression in Healing and Salvation," *Pastoral Psychology* 19 (September 1968): 33–39.

4. The pros and cons of this complicated debate are usefully summarized by C. Milo Connick, *Jesus, the Man, the Mission, and the Message* (Englewood Cliffs, N.J.: Prentice-Hall, 1974), 162–64. John P. Meier, *A Marginal Jew: Rethinking the Historical Jesus*, vol. 2, *Mentor, Message, and Miracles* (New York: Doubleday, 1994), summarily rejects this text from consideration in a study of the historical Jesus, since it "concerns Jesus' struggle with a preternatural being in the desert, with no eyewitnesses present" and is thus "in principle [not] open to verification" (p. 271). Of course, Jesus alone would have known of this experience, but he might have spoken of it to his disciples.

5. T. W. Manson, *The Servant-Messiah: A Study of the Public Ministry of Jesus* (Cambridge: Cambridge University Press, 1953, reissued by Baker Book House, 1977), poses a similar question: "Who in the Palestinian Christian community pictured in the first half of Acts could ever have invented this story?" (p. 55).

6. The opening sentence of "The Assumption of Moses," chapter 10, a first-century C.E. apocalyptic writing, reads as follows: "And then his [God's] kingdom shall appear throughout all his creation, And then Satan shall be no more, And sorrow shall depart with him." Quoted from *The New Testament Background: Selected Documents*, ed. C. K. Barrett (New York: Harper & Row, Harper Torchbook edition, 1961), 242.

7. Rudolf Bultmann, *History of the Synoptic Tradition*, rev. ed. (New York: Harper & Row, 1963), 256–57, states that "the Jewish tradition, though it certainly knew stories of temptation by Satan, knew of none about the temptation of Messiah, nor could it ever have recounted anything of this kind." See also the comments of Vernon McCasland, *The Pioneer of Our Faith*, 31, quoted at the beginning of this chapter.

8. The data bearing on this astonishing perspective is succinctly summarized by Ben Meyer, *The Aims of Jesus* (London: SCM, 1979), 155–57; see also James Kallas, *Jesus and the Power of Satan* (Philadelphia: Westminster Press, 1968).

9. For a somewhat similar argument in defense of the historical credibility of these temptation narratives, see J. Ramsey Michaels, *Servant and Son: Jesus in the Parable and Gospel* (Atlanta: John Knox, 1981), 63, and I. H. Marshall, *The Gospel of Luke: A Commentary on the Greek Text* (Grand Rapids: Eerdmans, 1979), 168.

10. Regarding these studies and the debates generated by them, see the section "Initial Questions" in the survey of psychological studies of Jesus in the Appendix.

11. T. W. Manson, *The Servant-Messiah*, summarizes this point of view succinctly when he writes that "we should regard it [the temptation narrative] as spiritual experience of Jesus thrown into parabolic narrative form for the instruction of his disciples" (p. 55).

12. On the nature and significance of metaphorical thought and its bearing

on the study of the parables, see especially John Dominic Crossan, *In Parables* (New York: Harper & Row, 1973), 10–22.

13. See Robert H. Stein, *Jesus the Messiah: A Survey of the Life of Christ* (Downers Grove: InterVarsity Press, 1996), 104, who believes this narrative is "spiritual autobiography" shared by Jesus with his disciples and as such does "not fit neatly into the categories of objective or subjective, external or internal."

14. Josephus writes in *The Jewish War*, Book VI, 312 (as translated in *Josephus: The Jewish War*, ed. Gaalya Cornfeld [Grand Rapids: Zondervan, 1982]), that the chief inducement for the Jewish rebellion against Rome in the years before the fall of Jerusalem in 70 C.E., was an "oracle also found in their sacred scriptures, announcing that at that time a man from their country would become ruler of the world." While Josephus is vague regarding the relevance of this oracle for an understanding of the various prophetic-messianic type revolutionaries he describes elsewhere as active during this period (see Book II, 118, 258–65), it is apparent that there must have been some connection. In Book II, 259, for example, these latter are described as "deceivers and imposters, claiming divine inspiration" and as men who "fostered revolutionary changes by inciting the mob to frenzied enthusiasm and by leading them into the wilderness under the belief that God would show them omens of freedom there." This is as plausible a background for understanding Jesus' wilderness temptations as one could hope for. On the shape of contemporary messianic ideology, see also Geza Vermes, *Jesus the Jew: A Historian's Reading of the Gospels* (New York: Macmillan, 1973), 130–34.

15. Regarding the coherence of the thoughts expressed here with Jesus' teachings elsewhere, see Michaels, *Servant and Son*, 61–63.

16. On the devil as a father figure, see Sigmund Freud, "A Neurosis of Demoniacal Possession in the Seventeenth Century," *Collected Papers*, vol. IV (London: The Hogarth Press, 1953), 436.

17. Erik Erikson, *Young Man Luther: A Study in Psychoanalysis and History* (New York: W. W. Norton, 1958), 59.

18. Ibid., 245.

19. Ibid, 247.

20. Freud, "Demoniacal Possession," 436–72.

21. Ibid., 446.

22. Ibid.

23. John Dominic Crossan, *In Fragments: The Aphorisms of Jesus* (San Francisco: Harper & Row, 1983), 18–36, notes that aphorisms of this type (and Jesus' aphorisms in particular) are deeply rooted in personal experience. Michaels, *Servant and Son*, observes that Jesus' saying about gaining the whole world and losing one's soul (Mark 8:36) "sounds curiously like an echo or reflection" of the third temptation (to worship Satan and thereby become a world ruler) (p. 48, n. 3).

24. For similar views, see Anton Boisen, *The Exploration of the Inner World:*

A *Study of Mental Disorder and Religious Experience* (Philadelphia: University of Pennsylvania Press, 1971; original ed., 1936); and Robert Leslie, *Jesus and Logotherapy* (New York: Abingdon Press, 1965), 13–23. For Boisen the story of the temptation in the wilderness is "indicative of a period of inner turmoil and mutation" in Jesus' life from which "he emerged victorious" and through which "he gained those insights which enabled him to speak with authority regarding the end and meaning of life and the laws of spiritual well-being" (p. 141). Leslie views the temptations as an ordeal during which Jesus repudiated instant gratification, the "power principle," and evasion of personal responsibility, "basic choices" confronting everyone who "steps from the shelter of the family into the arena of life" (p. 13).

Chapter 7

1. Schalom Ben-Chorin, *Bruder Jesus* (Munich: List Verlag, 1967), 129.
2. H.W. Montefiore, "Jesus, the Revelation of God," in *Christ for Us Today*, ed. N. Pittenger (London: SCM, 1968), 108–10.
3. John A. T. Robinson, *The Human Face of God* (London: SCM, 1973), 63f., 68, 70.
4. Montefiore, "Revelation of God," 109. See also Robert Wood, *Christ and the Homosexual* (New York: Vantage Press, 1960), 176, for a similar line of thought.
5. Noel I. Garde, *Jonathan to Gide* (New York: Vantage Press, 1964), 122–29.
6. Ibid., 124.
7. Ibid., 128f.
8. Tom Horner, *Jonathan Loved David: Homosexuality in Biblical Times* (Philadelphia: Westminster, 1978), 117. The prime candidate for some special relationship between Jesus and one of his male disciples has always been the "beloved disciple" referred to in the Gospel of John (13:23; 19:26; 20:2; 21:7, 20). Raymond Brown, *The Gospel according to John* I–XII (Garden City, N.Y.: Doubleday, 1966), believes this "beloved disciple" was John son of Zebedee (possibly a cousin of Jesus), and that the term "beloved disciple" was not one attributed to him by Jesus but by the "beloved disciple's disciples" (see pp. xciv, xcvi–xcviii).
9. Ben Witherington III, *Women in the Ministry of Jesus: A Study of Jesus' Attitudes to Women and Their Roles as Reflected in His Earthly Life* (Cambridge:Cambridge University Press, 1984), 31, makes the point that, in contrast to the Essenes of Qumran, Jesus' reference to celibacy "for the sake of the kingdom of heaven" appears to have "nothing to do with ritual purity or the idea that sexual relations made one impure."
10. It should be noted that Jesus' use of the term "one flesh" in this instance was not just a passing reference—an accident of the text he was citing, so to speak—but was singled out for special emphasis: "So they are no longer two," he

said a second time, "but one flesh" (Matt. 19:6//Mark 10:8f.). Witherington, *Women in the Ministry of Jesus*, correctly notes that "the implication is that the one flesh union becomes more constitutive of a man and woman's being than their uniqueness" (p. 26).

11. Quoted from Sigmund Freud, *Leonardo da Vinci: A Study in Psychosexuality* (New York: Vintage Books, 1916), 37.

12. David Dungan, *The Sayings of Jesus in the Churches of Paul* (Philadelphia: Fortress Press, 1971), 115–22, purports to have found in the Qumran literature analogies to Jesus' marital teachings, and remarks that it would be wrong to see in these "anything in the way of an idealization of the married estate, or of a profound appreciation of sexual union" (p. 118). However, so far as I know there is no text from Qumran that underscores (as does Jesus) the idea of "one flesh" as the basis for marital indissolubility. In this respect, Jesus goes well beyond Qumran in affirming the marital-sexual bond as a sacred sphere willed and sustained by God as creator—a point that Paul, among others, made fruitful in the early Christian congregations for which he was responsible (see 1 Cor. 7:1-16).

13. D. J. West, *Homosexuality*, 3d ed. (London: Gerald Duckworth & Co., 1968), 264. For a review of the research, see Lawrence J. Hatterer, *Changing Homosexuality in the Male* (New York: Dell Publishing Co., 1971), esp. 34–47, and Seymour Fisher and Roger Greenberg, *The Scientific Credibility of Freud's Theories and Therapy* (New York: Basic Books, 1977), 231–48.

14. Charles Socarides, "Abdicating Fathers, Homosexual Sons: Psychoanalytic Observations on the Contribution of the Father to the Development of Male Homosexuality," in *Father and Child*, ed. Stanley Cath et al. (Boston: Little, Brown and Co., 1982), 512. Socarides reports that two-thirds of the approximately four hundred men he studied during a ten-year period (1967–1977) were suffering from a type of homosexuality rooted in pre-oedipal experiences with "crushing" mothers and "abdicating" fathers. As a result "the boundary between self and object, the self and mother, is blurred or incomplete, with a resultant persistence of primary feminine identification with her and a disturbance in gender-defined self-identity" (p. 511).

15. Fisher and Greenberg, *The Scientific Credibility of Freud's Theories and Therapy*, 242.

16. André Gide, "Le Retour de l'Enfant Prodigue," in the *André Gide Reader*, ed. David Littlejohn (New York: Alfred A. Knopf, 1971), 379–93.

17. Ibid., 389.

18. William E. Phipps, *Was Jesus Married? The Distortion of Sexuality in the Christian Tradition* (New York: Harper & Row, 1971); see also his *The Sexuality of Jesus* (New York: Harper & Row, 1973), and Ben-Chorin, *Bruder Jesus* 127–30.

19. Phipps (*Was Jesus Married?* 33) quotes one rabbi who stated that "any man who has no wife lives without joy, without blessing, and without goodness" (Yevamoth 62b).

20. The one exception is the second-century Gnostic Gospel of Phillip. Regarding this, see Phipps, *Was Jesus Married?* 135–38.

21. After a thorough review of the evidence, John P. Meier, *A Marginal Jew*, vol. 1, *The Problem and the Person* (New York: Doubleday, 1991), 332–45, comes to the same conclusion; likewise Samuel Terrien, *Till the Heart Sings, A Biblical Theology of Manhood and Womanhood* (Philadelphia: Fortress Press, 1985), Terrien summarizes that since "the nascent church paid a great deal of attention to the family of Jesus," their failure to mention a wife must be significant and mean there was none (p. 124).

22. Regarding the traditional obligations of a Jewish father toward his sons and the eldest in particular see chapter 4.

23. The Talmud, Kiddushin 30a, reports rabbinic opinion as in favor of a father arranging such a marriage while the father still has control of his son, between his sixteeth and twenty-second year, with some preferring it be done a bit later (between eighteen and twenty-four). For a discussion of this issue, see Phipps, *Was Jesus Married?* 47.

24. Meier, *Marginal Jew*, vol. 1, 345, correctly distinguishes the meaning celibacy might have had in Jesus' life *before* and *after* the beginning of his public mission, but he questions the need for a hypothesis that would be explanatory of both. This is puzzling, since an explanation of Jesus' celibacy for the earlier years of his adult life is as important as for the brief period of his public mission, and the two are obviously related.

25. These two stories are sometimes viewed as variations on a single tradition, but the details are strikingly different.

26. The conversation between Jesus and a Samaritan woman, as recorded in John 4:4-42, is also sometimes included in the lists of episodes that are considered relevant to an understanding of Jesus' attitude toward women, but even the generally conservative Raymond Brown, *John* I–XII, can find no basis, in this instance, for defending its historicity (p. 175f.).

27. So writes the usually phlegmatic Joachim Jeremias, *New Testament Theology*, pt. 1, *The Proclamation of Jesus* (London: SCM, 1971), 227, and adds that "no where in the social sphere does the new life make so striking an incursion into everyday affairs as here."

28. Ben-Chorin, *Bruder Jesus*, 124. Witherington, *Women in the Ministry of Jesus*, believes that what made Jesus' conduct in this regard possible was his "rejection of rabbinic ideas of sin and sickness leading to ritual impurity or defilement" (also his implicit rejection of the idea that a blood-flow in a woman could defile her). This new attitude was perhaps also one of the factors that paved the way for women to travel with him and to be full-time followers (pp. 77f.).

29. Witherington (ibid., 50), states that there is nothing in Jesus' teaching that could be said to reject the patriarchal framework of his culture. His marital teaching, in fact, puts more, not less responsibility on the shoulders of men. "The net effect of Jesus' teaching on marriage and divorce is that the traditional family structure is not only reaffirmed but also strengthened through the intensification of the demands made on a husband's fidelity and the rejection of divorce outright."

30. There are three accounts of how these women may have been involved in Jesus' life: Luke 10:38-42; John 11:1-44; and John 12:1-11. For a thorough discussion of these texts, see again Witherington, ibid., 100–114. "Though it is unlikely they travelled with Jesus, Mary and Martha may have been the most important and prominent women in Jesus' life after His own mother" (p. 100).

31. On the growth of the legends regarding Mary Magdalene, see Leonard Swidler, *Biblical Affirmations of Woman* (Philadelphia: Westminster, 1979), 207–14.

32. For details on the Aramaic usage here, see Jeremias, *N.T. Theology*, 4, n. 9.

33. Geza Vermes, *Jesus the Jew, A Historian's Reading of the Gospels* (New York: Macmillan, 1973), 99–102; for an overview of Jewish attitudes toward celibacy and a similar conclusion, see Meier, *Marginal Jew*, vol. 1, 336–45.

34. To the list of Jesus' words calling men to exercise control over their wayward sexual feelings, Witherington, *Women in the Ministry of Jesus*, adds Jesus' saying in Matthew 5:29f. ("If your right eye causes you to sin, pluck it out . . . , if your right hand causes you to sin, cut it off . . ."), since loss of eye and hand were punishments actually meted out in the Palestine of that time for sexual misbehavior (p. 21).

35. For a contrary opinion see Paul Jewett, *Man as Male and Female: A Study in Sexual Relationships from a Theological Point of View* (Grand Rapids: Eerdmans, 1975), 110.

36. Robinson, *Face of God*, for example, thinks that were we to learn that Jesus was in fact homosexual, this would be of no greater consequence than if it were shown that he had been "snub-nosed" (p. 70).

37. Gordon Taylor, "Historical and Mythological Aspects of Homosexuality," in *Sexual Inversion: The Multiple Roots of Homosexuality*, ed. Judd Marmor (New York: Basic Books, 1965), 152.

38. Ibid., 153f. Further to the biblical, psychological, and cultural issues involved, see John W. Miller, *Biblical Faith and Fathering: Why We Call God "Father"* (New York: Paulist Press, 1989).

Chapter 8

1. Albert Nolan, *Jesus before Christianity* (London: Darton, Longman and Todd, 1976), 124.

2. See chapter 4 and the review of Besdine's research on this subject in the overview of "Psychoanalytic Perspectives" in the Appendix.

3. J. Marvin Eisenstadt, "Parental Loss and Genius," *American Psychologist* 33 (March 1978): 211–22.

4. See Ben Meyer, *The Aims of Jesus* (London: SCM, 1979), 158–68, for an excellent summing up of the evidence bearing upon Jesus' mission to this sector of his society.

5. Erikson's work is summarized in his famous essay, "Eight Ages of Man," in

Childhood and Society, 2d ed. (New York: W. W. Norton, 1963), 261–68, Levinson's in his *The Seasons of a Man's Life* (New York: Alfred Knopf, 1978).

6. Levinson, *Seasons of a Man's Life*, 322–40.

7. Ibid., 84–111.

8. Ibid., 91.

9. Ibid., 92.

10. Ibid., 99.

11. Ibid., 86.

12. This hypothesis becomes increasingly credible in the light of the considerable building activity we now realize was going on in Sepphoris during Jesus' young adulthood. For details on what is now known about the history of this major Galilean city, see Francis Boelter, "Sepphoris—Seat of the Galilean Sanhedrin," *Explor* 3 (Winter 1977): 36–43; Sean Freyne, *Galilee, Jesus and the Gospels, Literary Approaches and Historical Investigations* (Dublin: Gill and Macmillan, 1988), 135–75; Richard A. Batey, *Jesus and the Forgotten City: New Light on Sepphoris and the Urban World of Jesus* (Grand Rapids: Baker Book House, 1991).

13. Richard L. Bushman, "Jonathan Edwards as Great Man: Identity, Conversion and Leadership in the Great Awakening," in *Encounter with Erikson* (Missoula: Scholars Press, 1977), 217.

14. Erik Erikson, *Life History and the Historical Moment: Diverse Presentations* (New York: W. W. Norton, 1975), 22–47.

15. It is hard to imagine that either an early Christian or Baptist group would have invented the statement that "Jesus was making and baptizing more disciples than John" (4:1). The editorial addendum in 4:2 ("although Jesus himself did not baptize, but only his disciples") adds to this impression. Concerning the historical probability of this development and its place in the emergence of Jesus as a leader in his own right, see Joachim Jeremias, *New Testament Theology*, pt. 1, *The Proclamation of Jesus* (London: SCM, 1971), 45f.; Meyer, *Aims of Jesus*, 283, n. 23; according to Raymond Brown, *The Gospel according to John* I–XII (Garden City, N.Y.: Doubleday, 1966), 154f., these events belong to the very beginning stages of Jesus' relation with John, rather than where the Gospel of John now locates them.

16. E. P. Sanders, *Jesus and Judaism* (Philadelphia: Fortress Press, 1985), 186–211, emphasizes the importance of distinguishing between "sinners" and *'am ha-aretz* (common people); "sinners" were those who flagrantly and persistently disobeyed the law; the "common people" were simply lax. Aharon Oppenheimer, *The 'Am Ha-aretz: A Study in the Social History of the Jewish People in the Hellenistic-Roman Period* (Leiden: E. J. Brill, 1977), identifies two types of these latter. Some were criticized by the religious elite for their failure to eat secular food in ritual purity and to tithe properly (these were known as *'am ha-haretz le-mitzvot*), others for their ignorance of the Torah (these were referred to as *'am ha-aretz la-Torah*; p. 68f.). Perhaps these are the groups referred to in the

Gospels as "simple ones" (Matt. 11:25) or "little ones" (Mark 9:42; Matt. 10:42; 18:10, 14). "Tax collectors" were regarded as synonomous with "sinners" (Mark 2:16; Matt. 11:19; Luke 15:1), because the very nature of their jobs forced them to be lax toward Torah. Regarding this issue, see also William Farmer, *Jesus and the Gospel* (Philadelphia: Fortress Press, 1982), 31f.

17. Jacob Neusner, *Self-Fulfilling Prophecy: Exile and Return in the History of Judaism* (Boston: Beacon Press, 1977), 56.

18. For an especially terse and illuminating analysis and description of this ideology, see John Bowker, *Jesus and the Pharisees* (Cambridge: Cambridge University Press, 1973), 16. E. P. Sanders' catch-all term for this mode of religious life is "covenantal nomism." It was, he says, the form of religion that Jesus himself knew and accepted, even though he may not have put as much emphasis on "nomism"; see his *Jesus and Judaism*, p. 36.

19. David Rhoads, *Israel in Revolution 6–74* C.E., A *Political History Based on the Writings of Josephus* (Philadelphia: Fortress Press, 1976), 32–33, states that only a small minority of the five hundred thousand or so Jewish residents in Palestine belonged to the major sects; "the majority of Jews were the ordinary peasants of Israel, who were in general lukewarm about religion."

20. Regarding this practice, see Jeremias, *N.T. Theology*, 118f. Sanders, *Jesus and Judaism*, while arguing that the picture some scholars have drawn of a scribal elite banning these groups has been exaggerated, also admits "there were restrictions" (p. 192).

21. Marcus Borg, *Conflict, Holiness and Politics in the Teaching of Jesus* (Lewistown: Edwin Mellen, 1984), 69f.

22. M. Hengel, *The Charismatic Leader and His Followers* (New York: Crossroad, 1981), 36, notes that "the way the disciples of the Baptist, after their Master's death, developed into a messianic movement in competition with Christianity, and the identification of the Baptist in the Christian community with Elijah as the one who prepared the way for the Kingdom of God in terms of Malachi 3:22ff. suggests "that John understood himself not merely as the forerunner of the judge but alongside this as the mediator of salvation."

23. Hengel (ibid.), characterizes Jesus as "a man of his time, of his country, and of his people—a Jew from the Galilean 'people of the land'" (p. 39); Meier, *Marginal Jew*, vol. 1, emphasizes that he was a "Jewish layman" and not of priestly descent (pp. 345–49). On the issue of Jesus' own experience of alienation from God and personal need at the time of his baptism, see the discussion of this issue in chap. 3 of the present work.

24. Paul Hollenbach, "The Conversion of Jesus: From Jesus the Baptizer to Jesus the Healer," in *Aufstieg und Niedergang der römischen Welt: Geschichte und Kultur Roms im Spiegel der neueren Forschung II*, ed. Hildegard Temporini and Wolfgang Haase, (Berlin and New York: Walter de Gruyter, 1982), 204, hypothesizes that since Jesus became a coworker of John's (John 3:22-26; 4:1-3), he must have also been a disciple practicing "John's distinctive religious disci-

plines of dieting, fasting, and prayer." Meier states at the conclusion of his thorough review of the subject (*A Marginal Jew*, vol. 2, 116–23) that "John the Baptist, his message, his life, and his baptism are all to be seen as a vital and indispensable matrix of Jesus' own message and praxis" (p. 123).

25. Further to this Eriksonian category, see Don Browning, *Generative Man: Psychoanalytic Perspectives* (Philadelphia: Westminster, 1973), 145–217.

26. John 4:1 states that when Jesus learned that the Pharisees had heard that he "was making and baptizing more disciples than John . . . , he left Judaea and departed again to Galilee." According to Brown, *John* I–XII, 164f., this implies that Jesus' motive for returning to Galilee was his belief that the growing hostility toward him on the part of the Jerusalem-Pharisaic elite posed a danger. These same Pharisees had apparently already forced John into moving northward into Samaria (see John 3:23).

27. Regarding Jesus' break with John on fasting, see Matthew 9:14f. That Jesus ceased praying in the manner of John is implied by his gift to his disciples of a new prayer in response to their request that he teach them to pray as John "taught his disciples" (Luke 11:1). The contrast in dietary styles is alluded to by Jesus himself in Matthew. 11:18f. For an insightful discussion of these texts and their bearing on Jesus' relation to John at this stage of his mission, see again Hollenbach, "The Conversion of Jesus," 207–16. Meier, *Marginal Jew*, vol. 2, thinks it likely that Jesus continued baptizing, but that the memory of this was suppressed in the Synoptic tradition due to "theological embarrassment" (p. 126).

28. This possibility, initially suggested by C. H. Kraeling, *John the Baptist* (New York: Scribner, 1969), 148–50, is persuasively argued by Hollenbach, "The Conversion of Jesus," 209–17, who believes that an important factor in Jesus' break with John was his experience as exorcist. Meier, *Marginal Jew*, vol. 2, cautions against exaggerating this break or specifying its reasons, but agrees that after separating from John there were "notable shifts of emphasis in both his [Jesus'] preaching and his practice" (p. 124). I will have more to say below on the possible psychological dynamics involved (see esp. n. 48).

29. On this important issue, see Geza Vermes, *Jesus and the World of Judaism* (Philadelphia: Fortress Press, 1983), 47, who writes that "where the law is concerned, the chief distinction of Jesus' piety lies in his extraordinary emphasis on the real inner religious significance of the commandments . . . it is excretion that defiles, not ingestion and . . . nothing defiles more foully than the excretion of the wicked heart with its evil thoughts." Borg, *Conflict, Holiness and Politics*, argues similarly that whereas the other renewal movements of the time "intensified the Torah in the direction of holiness, emphasizing various forms of separation—from society as a whole, from the Gentiles, from impurity within society—Jesus intensified the Torah primarily by applying it to internal dimensions of the human psyche: to dispositions, emotions, thoughts and desires" (p. 238).

30. On recent thinking regarding the tension between present and future in the "kingdom of God" sayings of Jesus, see Dennis C. Duling, "Kingdom of

God, Kingdom of Heaven, New Testament and Early Christian Literature," *Anchor Bible Dictionary* IV (New York: Doubleday, 1992), 62–65. Based on the use of "kingdom of God" in Aramaic paraphrases of the Hebrew Bible (Targumim), Bruce Chilton, *Pure Kingdom: Jesus' Vision of God* (Grand Rapids: Eerdmans, 1996), believes that "the future-oriented, eschatological aspect of the kingdom" in Jesus' teachings is "to be acknowledged . . . , but it stems from Jesus' view of God, not from a particular (apocalyptic) expectation for the future." In other words, in Jesus' thought, "'the kingdom of God' fundamentally *is* God, as he manifests himself for his people" (pp. 11f.). Borg's view (*Conflict, Holiness and Politics*) is somewhat similar: "'Kingdom of God' was Jesus' designation or 'name' for the primordial beneficent power of the other realm, an energy which can become active in ordinary reality and which flows through him in his exorcisms" (pp. 253f.). The issue of how present and future might be related must have become increasingly urgent as Jesus faced the prospect of death. Regarding this, see below.

31. Borg, *Conflict, Holiness and Politics*, 246. For similar conclusions, see also John Bowker, *Jesus and the Pharisees* (Cambridge: Cambridge University Press, 1973), 43; Asher Finkel, *The Pharisees and the Teacher of Nazareth, A Study of Their Background, Their Halachic and Midrashic Teachings, the Similarities and Differences* (Leiden and Cologne: E. J. Brill, 1974), 133f., and Irving M. Zeitlin, *Jesus and the Judaism of His Time* (Cambridge: Polity Press, 1988), 158. Bowker writes that "Jesus did not necessarily deny the observance of Torah, . . . but he certainly resisted the view that the observance is an indispensable and prior condition of the action of God; faith is, if anything, the prior condition" (p. 43). Finkel believes Jesus deviated from the path of his contemporaries for the sake of his mission to "the lost sheep of the house of Israel" (pp. 133f.). Zeitlin stresses that although innovative in his challenge of specific traditions, "there is nothing in his words or deeds that should give anyone licence to read him out of Judaism" (p. 158).

32. On the role of Jesus' disciples as active "fellow-workers" in doing precisely what he did, see Hengel, *The Charismatic Leader*, 73–80.

33. The historicity of the appointment of "the Twelve" as a core feature of Jesus' identity and mission is defended by E. P. Sanders, *Jesus and Judaism*, 98–106. On the symbolic significance of this action, see Meyer, *Aims of Jesus*, p. 173, who believes that "restoration motifs" were thus evoked "that had stamped the hope of Israel since the days of Ezekiel (see Ezek. 47.13–48.29)" (p. 173). For the way Israelite hopes were inextricably linked to hope for the world in ancient Israelite thought (as in Gen. 12:3; Isa. 2:1-5; 49:6; 56:1-7; Jer. 3:16f.; Zech. 8:20-23; 2 Chron. 6:32f.; Sir. 36:16-19, et al.), see Isaac Rabinowitz, *A Witness Forever, Ancient Israel's Perception of Literature and the Resultant Hebrew Bible* ([Bethesda: CDL Press, 1993], 110–21).

34. Knowledgeable as Jesus was of the scriptures, his approach to this crisis was not primarily that of a scriptural exegete but, rather, he defended himself on the basis of metaphorical stories (parables) drawn from the experiences of daily

life, as, for example, when he asked whether a shepherd with a flock of one hundred sheep—of which one is lost—would not go looking for the one that was lost, and rejoice when he found it more than over the ninety-nine that were safe and secure (Luke 15:3-7). On the contrasts that can be drawn between Jesus' approach in this regard and that of the scribal elite of his time, see Hengel, *The Charismatic Leader*, 42–50.

35. The historicity of this association between Pharisees and Herodians in opposing Jesus (cf. Mark 12:13) is defended by Bowker, *Jesus and the Pharisees*, 41. According to Harold W. Hoehner, *Herod Antipas, A Contemporary of Jesus Christ* (Grand Rapids: Zondervan, 1980; repr. of 1972 ed. published by Cambridge University Press), 331–42, the Herodians were "men of standing and influence whose outlook was friendly to the Herodian rule and consequently to the Roman rule upon which that rested" (p. 332).

36. Regarding the importance of John's fate for Jesus' developing strategy, see T. W. Manson, *The Servant-Messiah: A Study of the Public Ministry of Jesus* (Grand Rapids: Baker Book House, 1977, first publ. in 1953), 41; Carl Kraeling, *John the Baptist* (New York: Scribner, 1951), 156f.

37. For exemplary studies of the way Jesus' religious critique intersected with his political critique, see John Piper, *Love Your Enemies*, Society for New Testament Studies, Monograph Series 38 (Cambridge: Cambridge University Press, 1979), 66–88; William Farmer, *Jesus and the Gospel* (Philadelphia: Fortress Press, 1982), 30–48; Borg, *Conflict, Holiness and Politics*, esp. 229–37.

38. Borg, *Conflict, Holiness and Politics*, 198. On the basis of passages such as Mark 13:2; Luke 13:1-5; Luke 13:34-35//Matt. 23:37-39; Luke 19:42-44, Borg argues that Jesus "appeared in history not only as a holy man with numinous powers who undertook a mission of renewal in the name of mercy, but also as a prophet who spoke of the consequences of his people's present course" (p. 198). For a similar conclusion, see Nolan, *Jesus before Christianity*, 17–18.

39. For a defense and elaboration of this aspect of Jesus' thought, see Joachim Jeremias, *Jesus' Promise to the Nations* (Philadelphia: Fortress Press, 1982; German ed., 1956); Eckhard J. Schnabel, "Jesus and the Beginnings of the Mission to the Gentiles," in *Jesus of Nazareth, Lord and Christ, Essays on the Historical Jesus and New Testament Christology*, ed. Joel B. Green and Max Turner (Grand Rapids: Eerdmans, 1994), 37–74 (esp. p. 54). Chilton, *Pure Kingdom*, while supporting the historicity of Jesus' saying about the temple being a house of prayer, questions the authenticity of "the specific assurance that 'all the nations' are to be included" by noting that it "is not to be found" in Matthew or Luke (Matt. 21:13; Luke 19:46) (p. 93). This omission may be due, however, to the post-resurrection emergence of an alternate vision of how Gentiles are going to learn of Israel's God (see Matt. 28:16-20; Luke 24:47; Acts 1:6-8).

40. For a defense of the historicity and intelligibility of this "esoteric tradition" (words spoken to disciples only), see Meyer, *Aims of Jesus*, 174–85; "Jesus Christ," *Anchor Bible Dictionary* III (New York: Doubleday, 1992), 792. Meyer believes the anticipated pilgrimage of the nations to Israel's temple was "the way

in which Jesus conceived of the Gentiles' entry into salvation" (*Aims*, 247). William Manson, *Jesus the Messiah* (London: Hodder and Stoughton, 1943), 160–65, drew similar conclusions as to the inner connections between Jesus' calling "to make the grace of God an instant and indefeasible reality in the lives of the 'lost sheep' of Israel" and his climactic hope-filled actions and words at the Temple and during his final meal with his disciples (p. 163).

41. Concerning the political factors generally that prompted Jesus' arrest and execution, see Ellis Rivkin, *What Crucified Jesus?* (Nashville: Abingdon, 1984), 36f. Rivkin writes that "in a world where violence stalked the countryside, death frequented the streets of Jerusalem, and riots disturbed the precincts of the Temple, where every flutter of dissidence sent chills of fear up the spines of puppet kings, governors, procurators, and procurator-appointed high priests—even the most nonpolitical of charismatics took his life in his hands when he preached the good news of God's coming kingdom."

42. On the controversial matter of whether Jesus' last meal with his disciples was on the day *before* Passover (as John's Gospel indicates) or on Passover day itself (as the Synoptics insist), see Brown, *John* I–XII, 555f., who argues for the pre-Passover date.

43. On the credibility of the "blasphemy" charge, see Darrell L. Bock, "The Son of Man Seated at God's Right Hand and the Debate over Jesus' 'Blasphemy,'" in *Jesus of Nazareth: Lord and Christ: Essays on the Historical Jesus and New Testament Christology*, ed. Joel B. Green and Max Turner (Grand Rapids: William B. Eerdmans, 1994), 181–91, who documents how offensive Jesus' saying about being "seated at the right hand of the power of God" (Luke 22:69) would have been, given the religious sensibilities of the time and "the leadership's past tensions with Jesus over issues related to who had authority to reveal God's way" (p. 191). That Jesus neither refuted nor accepted the charge of claiming to be the Messiah (as reported in Matt. 26:63f. and Luke 22:67-70) also seems credible, for the grandiose messianic stereotype he had so fiercely contested throughout his mission (see also below) was no longer at issue. Indeed, to let the charge stand under these circumstances (his trial and imminent death!) was ironical—an act of courage that drained this ascription of its prior meanings.

44. Hengel, *The Charismatic Leader*, 49. Ben Meyer, *The Aims of Jesus*, seems to agree: "His mission" is a "deft, assured, original foray into iniquity and redemption . . ." (p. 218). Hans Küng, *On Being a Christian* (Garden City, N.Y.: Doubleday, 1976), 212, concludes his discussion of the novelty of Jesus' mission by declaring that "despite all parallels in detail, the historical Jesus in his wholeness turns out to be completely unique—in his own time and ours."

45. For a cogent description of "Jesus as Sage" see Borg, *Conflict, Holiness and Politics*, 237–47.

46. On the importance of this relationship for Freud's self-discovery and scientific work, see Paul Roazen, *Freud and His Followers* (New York: New American Library, 1971), 88–96.

47. Erikson is quite candid on this point in his "Identity Crisis in Autobio-

graphical Perspective," in *Life History and the Historical Moment: Diverse Presentations* (New York: W. W. Norton, 1975), 29.

48. The mentor is invariably "a transitional figure," emphasizes Levinson, *The Seasons of a Man's Life*, due to the innate drive of the "age thirty" male to find himself and realize his destiny (p. 99). It would be a mistake, therefore, to single out one event or experience as the "root cause" of Jesus' eventual independence and differentiation from John, such as the "dis-confirmation" of John's eschatological expectations (John Riches, *Jesus and the Transformation of Judaism* [London: Darton, Longman and Todd, 1980], 165, 180) or his exorcisms (Kraeling, *John the Baptist*, 150f.; Hollenbach, "The Conversion of Jesus," 209–16). For a somewhat more detailed analysis of the relevance of Levinson's research for this facet of Jesus' life, see John W. Miller, "Jesus' 'Age Thirty Transition,' A Psychohistorical Probe," *Journal of Psychology and Christianity* 6/1 (Spring 1983): 19–29.

49. Scholarly discussion of this issue usually turns on whether Jesus did or did not think of himself as Messiah, with some thinking he did (for example, Ben Witherington III, *The Christology of Jesus* [Minneapolis: Fortress Press, 1990], 271) and others thinking he did not (for example, Vermes, *Jesus the Jew*, 145–49). What is often missing is recognition of how emotionally abhorrent the prevailing messianic idealizations were for him.

50. On the possibility that John the Baptist did actually, for a time, entertain the thought that Jesus might be the Messiah who would supersede him, see Hollenbach, "The Conversion of Jesus," 213.

51. Luke's version, in Luke 7:21-23, interprets this poetic allusion (based on Isa. 29:18-19) literally ("In that hour he cured many of the diseases and plagues and evil spirits, and on many that were blind he bestowed sight"); for a discussion of Luke's motives for doing this, see T. W. Manson, *The Sayings of Jesus* (Grand Rapids: Eerdmans, 1979 [first published as pt. 2 of *The Mission and Message of Jesus*, 1937]), 66.

52. Hollenbach, "The Conversion of Jesus," 213–17.

53. Joachim Jeremias, *The Prayers of Jesus* (Naperville: Allenson, 1967), 45, documents the "turning of the tide" in favor of the historicity of these important texts. On their meaning and importance, see also Jeremias, *N.T. Theology*, 57–59; James Dunn, *Jesus and the Spirit* (London: SCM, 1975), 27-34; Robert Hammerton-Kelly, *God the Father: Theology and Patriarchy in the Teaching of Jesus* (Philadelphia: Fortress Press, 1979), 77–81; Meyer, *Aims of Jesus*, 152. The Greek word *panta*, usually translated "all things" refers, Jeremias suggests, to the fullness of the revelation. The text does not explicitly say when this "revelation" was given, but the aorist ("has been delivered") points to a particular disclosure, perhaps the one received at the time of his baptism. "What Jesus wants to convey [through these words] in the guise of an everyday simile is this," Jeremias summarizes: "Just as a father talks to his son, just as he teaches him the letters of the Torah, just as he initiates him into the well-prepared secrets of his craft, just as he hides nothing from him and opens his heart

to him as to no-one else, so God has granted me knowledge of himself" (*N.T. Theology*, 60).

54. On the existential quality and centrality of this feature of Jesus' consciousness, see esp. Dunn, *Jesus and the Spirit*, 37–40, and Borg, *Conflict, Holiness and Politics*, 128. N. T. Wright, *Jesus and the Victory of God* (Minneapolis: Fortress Press, 1996), also writes of Jesus' "particular intimacy with the one he called 'father' . . . as the inside of the picture" he has drawn of him, "giving depth to all the rest" (p. 650).

55. According to Jeremias "the only title used by Jesus of himself whose authenticity is to be taken seriously" is "Son of Man" (*N.T. Theology*, 258), but Vermes (*Jesus the Jew*, 160–91; *Jesus and the World of Judaism*, 89–99) has argued that even this was not a title in the world of Jesus but an idiom (Aramaic: *bar enash*) meaning "man," "some one," or a circumlocution for "I" in certain circumstances. For the way "Son of Man" entered the stream of early christology, see Borg, *Conflict, Holiness, and Politics*, 221–27. A title applied to Jesus by others, which he seemingly did not object to, is "David's son" (Matt. 20:29-32//Mark 10:46-52//Luke 18:35-43). It may be that the Davidic descent of his family was common knowledge (Matt. 1:1-17; Luke 3:23-38; Rom. 1:3). This might have a bearing on his refutation that a messianic claim was involved (Matt. 22:41-46//Mark 12:35-37//Luke 20:41-44). Regarding this, see Bruce Chilton, "Jesus *Ben David*: Reflections on the *Davidssohnfrage*," *The Historical Jesus, A Sheffield Reader*, ed. Craig A. Evans and Stanley E. Porter (Sheffield: Sheffield Academic Press, 1995), 192–215; repr. from *Journal for the Study of the New Testament* 14 (1982): 88–112.

56. The assumption that Jesus is reserving the titles referred to in this text (Rabbi, Father, Master) for *himself* is not credible if, as Matthew's context implies, he said this in criticism of love of titles among the religious elite. In that case, Jesus would be criticizing others for a form of vanity and self-display of which he himself was guilty. Nolan is therefore correct in observing that it is "quite obvious that the original intention of the sayings was that God alone was. . . Teacher, Father, and Master" (*Jesus before Christianity*, 120), even though the addendum to Matt. 23:10 (". . . for you have one master, the Christ") indicates that early Christians did understand it as having a christological relevance.

57. According to Edward Schillebeeckx, *Jesus: An Experiment in Christology* (New York: Seabury, 1979), 303–6, the "servant motif" in the Gospel portraits of Jesus is rooted not in Jesus' conscious appropriation of some scriptural prototype, but in his naturally humble role at communal meals with his disciples. The question arises as to how it happened that "Messiah" came so quickly to be associated with him in the early church, almost as a second name. Clearly, his disciples regarded him as such early on (John 1:41) but for this very reason were often at odds with him (Mark 10:35-45) because of the superhuman expectations associated with the form that "messianic" hopes had taken in their time (Luke 24:21; Acts 1:6; cf. Psalms of Solomon 17:23–77). Others regarded him as

a messianic pretender (Mark 15:26//Matt. 27:37). Only after his crucifixion and resurrection were these inflated hopes gradually abandoned in favor of a vision and mission more in line with the one he had espoused (Acts 1:6-8; Matt. 28:16-20). Thus, "Messiah" was a term of accusation and false expectation" before it was put to use as an expression of the church's emergent faith (Hengel, *The Charismatic Leader*, 39).

58. Commenting on these texts, Jeremias, *The Prayers of Jesus*, writes that with Jesus "a new way of praying is born. Jesus talks to his Father as naturally, as intimately and with the same sense of security as a child talks to his father" (p. 78).

59. Further on the way in which Jesus' parables convey not only his message but his manner and person, see John W. Miller, "Jesus' Personality as Reflected in His Parables," in *The New Way of Jesus*, ed. William Klassen (Newton: Faith and Life, 1980), 56–72. One exception to this use of parabolic figures in defense of his mission should be noted: the appeal to the example of David in the controversy over his disciples plucking grain on the sabbath (Matt. 12:3f.//Mark 2:25f.//Luke 6:3f.). On the "Davidic factor" as a feature of his consciousness, see n. 55 above.

60. On the programmatic sweep and importance of the saying "Be merciful, even as your Father is merciful," see Borg, *Conflict, Holiness, and Politics*, 123–34. For an especially profound discussion of Jesus' "Abba-experience" as "source and secret of his being, message, and manner of life," see Schillebeeckx, *Jesus*, 256–71.

Chapter 9

1. Erik Erikson, *Gandhi's Truth* (New York: W. W. Norton, 1969), 399.
2. Ibid., 399.
3. Ibid.
4. How different Jesus' inner world (as we know it from our earliest and historically most reliable sources) is from the kind of introverted, alienated, grandiose thoughts we now know those to have who, tragically (for whatever reason), cannot break free of a schizoid disorder, can be very quickly sensed by reading the vivid account of people so conflicted in a book like Shirley Sugerman's *Sin and Madness: Studies in Narcissism* (Philadelphia: Westminster, 1976), 128–47.
5. Pope John XXIII, *Journal of a Soul* (Montreal: Palm Publishers, 1965), 187.
6. Ibid., xvii.
7. Clifford Green, "Bonhoeffer in the Context of Erikson's Luther Study," in *Psychohistory and Religion: The Case of Young Man Luther*, ed. Roger Johnson (Philadelphia: Fortress Press, 1977), 162–96.
8. Ibid., 169.
9. Ibid., 186.

10. For a graphic description of Hitler's grandiosity and the developmental dynamics involved, see Walter C. Langer, *The Mind of Adolf Hitler* (New York: The New American Library, 1972).

11. On this way of viewing Jesus' significance, see Michael Goulder, "Jesus, the Man of Universal Destiny," in *The Myth of God Incarnate*, ed. John Hick (Philadelphia: Westminster, 1978), 48–63.

Appendix

1. Albert Schweitzer, *The Psychiatric Study of Jesus* (Boston: Beacon Press, 1948), 28.

2. John McIntyre, "The Psychological Model," in *The Shape of Christology* (London: SCM, 1966), 124–43, notes that in rejecting the nineteenth-century "psychologizing" of Jesus, many historians give the impression that *nothing at all* can be known about Jesus in this regard, even though these same scholars go on to speak of recovering a more accurate picture of Jesus' "personality." Also Don Browning, "The Influence of Psychology on Theology," in *The New Shape of Pastoral Theology: Essays in Honor of Seward Hiltner*, ed. William B. Oglesby, Jr. (Nashville: Abingdon, 1969), 121–35, points out that leading modern theologians (Bultmann and Tillich) are already using a psychology of sorts—existentialism—in their interpretation of Jesus, although it is one that lacks a "phenomenology of genesis" and is therefore incapable of recognizing the fact that some of the structures of consciousness may have a developmental history. An exception to the neglect of this subject among biblical scholars is Vincent Taylor's chapter on "Christology and Psychology," in his classic work *The Person of Christ in New Testament Teaching* (London: Macmillan, 1958), 277–85.

3. The classic survey of the nineteenth-century facet of this history is still Albert Schweitzer's *The Quest of the Historical Jesus: A Critical Study of Its Progress from Reimarus to Wrede* (New York: Macmillan Paperback Edition, 1961; first German ed., 1906). For a general overview, see Warren Kissinger, *The Lives of Jesus: A History and Bibliography* (New York: Garland, 1985); Craig A. Evans, *Life of Jesus Research: An Annotated Bibliography*, rev. ed. (Leiden, New York, and Cologne: E. J. Brill, 1996). For the story of the quest in the twentieth century, with special emphasis on developments since 1960, see Gustaf Aulén, *Jesus in Contemporary Historical Research* (Philadelphia: Fortress Press, 1976), and John Hayes, *Son of God to Super Star: Twentieth Century Interpretations of Jesus* (Nashville: Abingdon, 1976). For a review of the renewed interest in the Jesus of history during the 1980s and 90s, see Ben Witherington III, *The Jesus Quest: The Third Search for the Jew of Nazareth* (Downers Grove: InterVarsity Press, 1995).

4. This controversy is reviewed and analyzed with considerable thoroughness by Walter E. Bundy, *The Psychic Health of Jesus* (New York: Macmillan, 1922) and G. Stanley Hall, *Jesus Christ in the Light of Psychology* (New York and London: D. Appleton, 1924).

5. For a recent English edition of this classic, see D. F. Strauss, *The Life of*

Jesus Critically Examined, ed. Peter Hodgson, Lives of Jesus Series (Philadelphia: Fortress Press, 1972).

6. Ibid., 296.

7. Ibid., xliv.

8. On this development, see Bundy, *Health of Jesus*, 2–7.

9. Ernest Renan, *Life of Jesus* (New York: Howard Wilford Bell, 1904), 229. Renan added that "sometimes one would have said that his reason seemed affected. He suffered mental anguish and agitation" (p. 230).

10. An example would be P. J. Moebius's study of Rousseau, *J. J. Rousseau's Krankheitsgeschichte* (Leipzig: G. C. W. Vogel, 1889), which gathers evidence from Rousseau's later years for a diagnosis that he suffered from a progressively degenerative "paranoia." On these developments in psychiatry, see F. Alexander and S. Selesnick, *The History of Psychiatry* (New York and Toronto: The New American Library, 1966), 196–224.

11. Johannes Weiss, *Jesus' Proclamation of the Kingdom of God*, ed. L. E. Keck, Lives of Jesus Series (Philadelphia: Fortress Press, 1971).

12. Published in English as *The Quest of the Historical Jesus* in 1910.

13. George Lomer [George de Loosten], *Jesus Christus vom Standpunkte des Psychiaters* (Bamberg: Handels-Druckerei, 1905).

14. Emil Rasmussen, *Eine vergleichende psychopathologische Studie* (Leipzig: Julius Zeitler, 1905).

15. William Hirsch, *Religion and Civilization: The Conclusions of a Psychiatrist* (New York: The Truth Seeker Co., 1912).

16. Ibid., 107, 137.

17. For an extensive review of these volumes, see Bundy, *Health of Jesus*, 85–107.

18. Ibid., 220.

19. Albert Schweitzer, *The Psychiatric Study of Jesus* (Boston: Beacon Press, 1948).

20. Ibid., 63.

21. Ibid., 65.

22. W. Overholser, "Foreword," in Schweitzer, *The Psychiatric Study of Jesus*, 15.

23. Anton Boisen, *The Exploration of the Inner World: A Study of Mental Disorder and Religious Experience* (Willett, Clark & Co., 1936; repr. ed., Philadelphia: University of Pennsylvania Press, 1971), 125–41.

24. Ibid., 139.

25. Boisen, "What Did Jesus Think of Himself?" *Journal of Bible and Religion* (January 1952): 11.

26. Ibid., 9.

27. For Freud's own final succinct summary of the Oedipus Complex and its importance, see *An Outline of Psycho-Analysis*, rev. ed. (New York: W. W. Norton, 1949), 40–51. The research in support of Freud's conclusions in this regard is reviewed by Seymour Fisher and Roger Greenberg, *The Scientific Credibility*

of Freud's Theories and Therapy (New York: Basic Books, 1977), 170–230.

28. A notable example would be Freud's *Leonardo da Vinci: A Study in Psychosexuality* (New York: Vintage Books, 1916).

29. Erik Erikson's studies of Gandhi, *Gandhi's Truth: On the Origins of Militant Nonviolence* (New York: W. W. Norton, 1969) and Luther, *Young Man Luther: A Study in Psychoanalysis and History* (New York: W. W. Norton, 1958), are the generally recognized "classics" of modern psychohistorical research. On the growth of research in this field and Erikson's and Levinson's contributions in particular, see chapters 1 and 8 of the present work.

30. Georges Berguer, *Some Aspects of the Life of Jesus from the Psychological and Psychoanalytic Point of View* (New York: Harcourt, Brace and Company, 1923).

31. Ibid., 146.

32. Ibid., 223.

33. Ibid., 247–55. Berguer's idea is that Jesus' own pure resolution of the Oedipus Complex functions as an exemplary force by means of which "the baser elements" of human personality are gradually being converted and transformed.

34. *British Journal of Medical Psychology* 21 (1947): 75–79.

35. Ibid., 76.

36. Ibid., 75.

37. Ibid., 77.

38. Ibid., 78.

39. Ibid., 77.

40. Ibid., 78.

41. Ibid., 78f.

42. R. S. Lee, *Freud and Christianity* (Harmondsworth, Middlesex, England: Penguin, 1948), 109.

43. Ibid., 167.

44. Matthew Besdine, "The Jocasta Complex, Mothering and Genius: Part I," *Psychoanalytic Review* 55 (Summer 1968): 259–77; "The Jocasta Complex: Part II," *Psychoanalyic Review* 55 (1968–69): 574–600; "Mrs. Oedipus," *Psychology Today* 2 (January 1969): 40–47, 67; "Mrs. Oedipus Has Daughters, Too," *Psychology Today* 4 (March 1971): 62–65, 99.

45. In Freud's initial analysis of oedipal dynamics, his attention was primarily on the emotional dynamic between son and *father*. Even when he drew the mother into the orbit of his reflections, it was primarily the role of the son that came into view, not that of the mother. Besdine is not alone among contemporary psychoanalysts in noticing this blind spot in Freud. On this issue, see, for example, Erich Fromm, *The Heart of Man: Its Genius for Good and Evil* (New York: Harper & Row, 1964), 96–113.

46. Besdine, "Mrs. Oedipus Has Daughters, Too," 99.

47. Besdine, "Mrs. Oedipus," 67.

48. A revival of interest in this topic may be indicated by Paul C. Vitz and John Gartner's essay, "Christianity and Psychoanalysis, Part 1: Jesus as the Anti-Oedipus," *Journal of Psychology and Theology* 12 (1984): 4–14, where Jesus' life

is described as "a perfect inversion of the behavior of the primitive horde—the original band of brothers. . . . Jesus shows not intense hate but perfect love for God the Father" (p. 8). Erik Erikson's seminal essay on this theme should also be mentioned, "The Galilean Sayings and the Sense of 'I'," *The Yale Review* 70 (Spring 1981): 321–62, in which he asks what concept of self, God, and others is in evidence in those sayings of Jesus adjudged by scholars to be authentic and from the earliest period of Jesus' mission. The noted psychologist David Bakan has also touched on this topic (the psychology of Jesus) in the closing pages of *The Duality of Human Existence, An Essay on Psychology and Religion* (Chicago: Rand McNally, 1966), 221–26. A series of meditations on several Gospel stories by two French psychoanalysts, Françoise Dolto and Gérard Sévérin, in their book *The Jesus of Psychoanalysis: A Freudian Interpretation of the Gospel* (New York: Doubleday, 1979), is not meant to be a contribution to an understanding of the Jesus of history, but rather an indication of the kinds of thoughts that come to mind as contemporary Christian psychoanalysts read the Gospels (or hear them read) just as they are.

49. On the earlier phases of this debate, see J. A. C. Brown, *Freud and the Post-Freudians* (Harmondsworth, Middlesex, England: Penguin, 1961). For a survey of the more recent schools of thought, see Raymond Corsini, *Current Psychotherapies* (Itasca, Ill.: P. E. Peacock, 1973). For a critique of these developments, see Russel Jacoby, *Social Amnesia: A Critique of Contemporary Psychology from Adler to Laing* (Boston: Beacon Press, 1975).

50. Jay Haley, *The Power Tactics of Jesus Christ* (New York: Avon, 1969).

51. Raymond Lloyd, "Cross and Psychosis, Part 1," *Faith and Freedom* (Fall 1970): 13–29; "Cross and Psychosis, Part 2," *Faith and Freedom* (Spring 1971): 67–87.

52. Edward Edinger, *Ego and Archetype* (New York: Putnam, 1972). A similar approach is taken by John A. Sanford, "Jesus, Paul, and Depth Psychology," in *Religious Education* 68 (1963): 673–89, and *The Kingdom Within* (Philadelphia: J. B. Lippincott, 1970); also Hanna Wolfe, *Jesus der Mann: Die Gestalt Jesu in tiefenpsychologischer Sicht* (Stuttgart: Radius, 1975).

53. Rosemary Haughton, *The Liberated Heart* (New York: Seabury, 1974), 173.

54. Donald Capps, "The Desire to Be Another Man's Son: The Child Jesus as an Endangered Self," in *The Endangered Self*, ed. Richard K. Fenn and Donald Capps, Monograph Series 2, Center for Religion, Self and Society (Princeton Theological Seminary, 1992), 21–35.

55. Robert Leslie, *Jesus and Logotherapy: The Ministry of Jesus as Interpreted through the Psychotherapy of Viktor Frankl* (Nashville: Abingdon, 1965).

56. Jon Buell and O. Quentin Hyder, *Jesus: God, Ghost or Guru* (Grand Rapids: Zondervan, 1978), 99; David L. McKenna pursues a somewhat similar line of thought in his book *The Jesus Model* (Waco, Tex.: Word Books, 1977).

57. On this see again McIntyre, "The Psychological Model," in *Shape of Christology* (n. 2 above).

Bibliography

Historical Jesus Studies

Barclay, William. *The Mind of Jesus.* London: SCM, 1960.

Barrett, C. K. *New Testament Background: Selected Documents.* New York: Harper & Row, Torchbook edition, 1961.

——— . *The Gospel According to St. John.* London: S.P.C.K., 1962.

Batey, Richard A. *Jesus and the Forgotten City: New Light on Sepphoris and the Urban World of Jesus.* Grand Rapids: Baker Book House, 1991.

Ben-Chorin, Schalom. *Bruder Jesus: Der Nazarener in jüdischer Sicht.* Munich: List Verlag, 1967.

Boelter, Francis. "Sepphoris—Seat of the Galilean Sanhedrin." *Explor* 3 (Winter 1977): 36–43.

Boobyer, C. H. "Jesus as 'Theos' in the New Testament." *Bulletin of the John Rylands Library* (January 1969): 247–61.

Borg, Marcus J. *Conflict, Holiness and Politics in the Teaching of Jesus.* Lewistown, N.Y.: Edwin Mellen, 1984.

———. *Jesus, A New Vision, Spirit, Culture, and the Life of Discipleship.* San Francisco: Harper & Row, 1987.

———. *Jesus in Contemporary Scholarship.* Valley Forge: Trinity Press International, 1994.

———. *Meeting Jesus Again for the First Time.* San Francisco: Harper-SanFrancisco, 1995.

Boring, Eugene. "Criteria of Authenticity, The Lucan Beatitudes as a Test Case." *Forum*, 1/4 (December 1985): 3–38.

Bornkamm, Günther. *Jesus of Nazareth*. New York: Harper and Brothers, 1960.

Bowker, John. *Jesus and the Pharisees*. Cambridge: Cambridge University Press, 1973.

Braun, Herbert. *Jesus of Nazareth: The Man and His Time*. Philadelphia: Fortress Press, 1979; German edition, 1969.

Breech, James. *The Silence of Jesus, The Authentic Voice of the Historical Man*. Philadelphia: Fortress Press, 1983.

Brown, Raymond. *The Gospel According to John*, I–XII, The Anchor Bible 29. Garden City, N.Y.: Doubleday, 1966.

——. *The Birth of the Messiah*. Garden City, N.Y.: Doubleday, 1977.

Buchanan, George Wesley. "Jesus and the Upper Classes." *Novum Testamentum* 7 (1964–65): 195–209.

——. *Jesus, The King and His Kingdom*. Macon: Mercer University Press, 1984.

Bultmann, Rudolf. *History of the Synoptic Tradition*. Revised edition. New York: Harper & Row, 1963.

——. *Jesus and the Word*. New York: Scribner, 1958.

Cadbury, Henry. *Jesus, What Manner of Man?* London: S.P.C.K., 1947.

Charlesworth, James H. "From Barren Mazes to Gentle Rappings: The Emergence of Jesus Research." *The Princeton Seminary Bulletin* VII/3 (New Series 1986): 221–30.

——. *Jesus within Judaism, New Light from Exciting Archaeological Discoveries*. New York: Doubleday, 1988.

Chilton, Bruce. "Jesus *ben David*: Reflections on the *Davidsohnfrage*." In *The Historical Jesus, A Sheffield Reader*, edited by Craig A. Evans and Stanley E. Porter 192–218. Sheffield: Sheffield Academic Press, 1995; first published in the *Journal for the Study of the New Testament* 14 (1982): 88–112.

——. *Pure Kingdom: Jesus' Vision of God*. Grand Rapids: William B. Eerdmans, 1996.

Connick, C. Milo. *Jesus, the Man, the Mission, and the Message*. 2d edition. Englewood Cliffs, N.J.: Prentice-Hall, 1974.

Cornfeld, Gaalya, ed. *The Historical Jesus, A Scholarly View of the Man and His World*. New York: Macmillan; London: Collier Macmillan, 1982.

Crossan, John Dominic. *The Historical Jesus, The Life of a Mediterranean Jewish Peasant.* San Francisco: HarperSanFrancisco, 1991.

——— . *In Fragments, The Aphorisms of Jesus*. San Francisco: Harper & Row, 1983.

——— . *In Parables*. New York: Harper & Row, 1973.

——— . *Jesus, A Revolutionary Biography*. San Francisco: HarperSanFrancisco, 1994.

——— . "Mark and the Relatives of Jesus." *Novum Testamentum* 15 (1973): 81–113.

Cupitt, Don. "The Christ of Christendom." In *The Myth of God Incaruate*, edited by John Hick, 133–47. London: SCM, 1977.

De Boer, Martinus C. ed. *From Jesus to John: Essays on Jesus and New Testament Christology, in Honour of Marinus de Jonge. Journal for the Study of the New Testament*, Supplement Series 84. Sheffield: Sheffield Academic Press, 1993.

Dodd, C. H. *The Founder of Christianity*. New York: Macmillan, 1970.

Duling, Dennis. "Kingdom of God, Kingdom of Heaven, New Testament and Early Christian Literature." *Anchor Bible Dictionary* IV, 56–69. New York: Doubleday, 1992.

Dungan, David. *The Teachings of Jesus in the Churches of Paul.* Philadelphia: Fortress Press, 1971.

Dunn, James. *Jesus and the Spirit*. London: SCM, 1975.

Evans, Craig A. *Life of Jesus Research, An Annotated Bibliography*. Revised edition. Leiden, New York and Cologne: E. J. Brill, 1996.

Evans, Craig A., and Stanley E. Porter, eds. *The Historical Jesus, A Sheffield Reader.* Sheffield: Sheffield Academic Press, 1995.

Eusebius. *The History of the Church from Christ to Constantine*. Translated by G. A. Williamson. Minneapolis: Augsburg, 1965.

Farmer, William. *Jesus and the Gospel, Tradition, Scripture and Canon.* Philadelphia: Fortress Press, 1982.

Faxon, Alicia Craig. *Women and Jesus.* Philadelphia: United Church Press, 1973.

Finkel, Asher. *The Pharisees and the Teacher of Nazareth.* Leiden and Cologne: E. J. Brill, 1974.

Flusser, David. *Jesus*. New York: Herder and Herder, 1969.

Freyne, Sean. *Galilee, Jesus and the Gospels, Literary Approaches and Historical Investigations.* Dublin: Gill and Macmillan, 1988.

Gaston, Lloyd. *No Stone on Another, Studies in the Significance of the Fall of Jerusalem in the Synoptic Gospels*. Leiden: E. J. Brill, 1970.

Gerhardsson, B. *The Testing of God's Son*. Lund, Sweden: CWK Gleerup, 1966.

Green, Joel B., and Max Turner, eds. *Jesus of Nazareth Lord and Christ. Essays on the Historical Jesus and New Testament Christology*. Grand Rapids: William B. Eerdmans, 1994.

Gray, Donald. "Was Jesus a Convert?" *Religion in Life* 43 (Winter 1974): 445–55.

Guignebert, Charles. *Jesus*. New York: University Books, 1956.

Hamerton-Kelly, Robert. *God the Father, Theology and Patriarchy in the Teaching of Jesus*. Philadelphia: Fortress Press, 1979.

Harvey, Van A. *The Historian and the Believer*. Toronto: Macmillan, 1969.

Hayes, John. *Son of God to Super Star, Twentieth Century Interpretations of Jesus*. Nashville: Abingdon, 1976.

Hengel, Martin. *The Charismatic Leader and His Followers*. New York: Crossroad, 1981; original German edition, 1968.

Hennecke, E. *New Testament Apocrypha* I, edited by W. Schneemelcher. London: SCM, 1963.

Hoehner, Harold W. *Herod Antipas, A Contemporary of Jesus Christ*. Grand Rapids: Zondervan, 1980; reprint of the 1972 edition published by Cambridge University Press.

Hollenbach, Paul. "The Conversion of Jesus: From Jesus the Baptizer to Jesus the Healer." *Aufstieg und Niedergang der römischen Welt; Geschichte und Kultur Roms in Spiegel der neueren Forschung II*, edited by Hildegard Temporini and Wolfgang Haase, Berlin and New York: Walter deGruyter, 1982.

Jeremias, Joachim. *Jerusalem in New Testament Times*. London: SCM, 1969.

———. *Jesus' Promise to the Nations*. Philadelphia: Fortress Press edition, 1982; first German edition, 1956.

———. *New Testament Theology*. Part 1, *The Proclamation of Jesus*. London: SCM, 1971.

———. *The Parables of Jesus*. Revised edition. London: SCM, 1963.

———. *The Prayers of Jesus*. Naperville: Allenson, 1967.

Josephus. *Josephus, The Jewish War, Newly translated with extensive com-*

mentary and archaeological background illustrations. Edited by Gaalya Cornfeld. Grand Rapids: Zondervan, 1982.

Kallas, James. *Jesus and the Power of Satan*. Philadelphia: Westminster, 1968.

Keck, Leander. *A Future for the Historical Jesus*. Grand Rapids: Eerdmans, 1977.

Kelso, James. *An Archaeologist Looks at the Gospels*. Waco and London: Word Books, 1969.

Kissinger, Warren. *The Lives of Jesus: A History and Bibliography*. New York: Garland, 1985.

Klausner, Joseph. *Jesus of Nazareth: His Life, Times and Teaching*. New York: Macmillan, 1926.

Kraeling, Carl H. *John the Baptist*. New York: Charles Scribner's Sons, 1969.

Küng, Hans. *On Being a Christian*. New York: Doubleday, 1976.

Lambrecht, J. "The Relatives of Jesus in Mark." *Novum Testamentum* 16 (1974): 241–58.

McCasland, Vernon S. *The Pioneer of Our Faith: A New Life of Jesus*. New York: McGraw-Hill, 1964.

McIntyre, John. *The Shape of Christology*. London: SCM, 1966.

Machovec, Milan. *A Marxist Looks at Jesus*. Philadelphia: Fortress Press, 1976.

Mackey, James. *Jesus the Man and the Myth: A Contemporary Christology*. New York and Ramsey: Paulist Press, 1979.

Manson, T. W. *The Servant-Messiah, A Study of the Public Ministry of Jesus*. Cambridge: Cambridge University Press, 1953; paperback edition issued 1977 by Baker Book House.

——— . *The Sayings of Jesus*. Grand Rapids: Eerdmans, 1979; first published in 1937 as Part 2 of *The Mission and Message of Jesus*.

Manson, William. *Jesus the Messiah*. London: Hodder and Stoughton, 1943.

Maritain, Jacques. *On the Humanity and Grace of Jesus*. New York: Herder and Herder, 1969.

Marshall, I. H. *The Gospel of Luke: A Commentary on the Greek Text*. Grand Rapids: Eerdmans, 1979.

Meier, John P. *A Marginal Jew: Rethinking the Historical Jesus*. Vol. 1, *The Problem and the Person*. New York: Doubleday, 1991.

——— . *A Marginal Jew, Rethinking the Historical Jesus*. Vol. 2, *Mentor, Message, and Miracles*. New York: Doubleday, 1994.

Meyer, Ben. *The Aims of Jesus*. London: SCM, 1979.

——— . "Jesus Christ." In *The Anchor Bible Dictionary* III. New York: Doubleday, 1992.

Michaels, J. Ramsey. *Servant and Son: Jesus in Parable and Gospel*. Atlanta: John Knox, 1981.

Milgrom, J. "First-born." In *The Interpreter's Dictionary of the Bible*, Supplementary Volume, edited by Keith Crim, 337–38. Nashville: Abingdon, 1976.

Miller, John W. *Step by Step through the Parables*. New York and Ramsey: Paulist Press, 1981.

Mitton, Leslie. *Jesus, The Fact behind the Faith*. Grand Rapids: Eerdmans, 1974.

Montefiore, H. W. "Jesus, The Revelation of God." In *Christ for Us Today*, edited by N. Pittenger, 101–16. London: SCM, 1968.

Murry, J. Middleton. *Jesus, Man of Genius*. New York: Harper & Brothers, 1926.

Neusner, Jacob. *The Rabbinic Traditions about the Pharisees before 70*. Part 1. Leiden: E. J. Brill, 1971.

——— . *Judaism in the Beginning of Christianity*. Philadelphia: Fortress Press, 1982.

——— . *Self-fulfilling Prophecy, Exile and Return in the History of Judaism*. Boston: Beacon Press, 1987).

Nolan, Albert. *Jesus before Christianity*. London: Darton, Longman and Todd, 1976.

O'Collins, Gerald. *What Are They Saying about Jesus?* New York: Paulist Press, 1977.

Oppenheimer, Ahron. *The 'Am Ha-Aretz, A Study in the Social History of the Jewish People in the Hellenistic-Roman Period*. Arbeiten zur Literatur und Geschichte des hellenistischen Judentums 8. Leiden: E. J. Brill, 1977.

Pelikan, Jaroslav. *Jesus through the Centuries, His Place in the History of Culture*. New Haven and London: Yale University Press, 1985.

Phipps, William E. *Was Jesus Married?* New York: Harper & Row, 1971.

——— . *The Sexuality of Jesus*. New York: Harper & Row, 1973.

Piper, John. *Love Your Enemies*. Society for New Testament Studies, Monograph Series 38. Cambridge: Cambridge University Press, 1979.

Pokorny', Petr. "The Temptation Stories and Their Intention." *New Testament Studies* 20 (1973–74): 115–27.

Rhoads, David. *Israel in Revolution, 6–74* C.E. Philadelphia: Fortress Press, 1976.

Riches, John. *Jesus and the Transformation of Judaism.* London: Darton, Longman and Todd, 1980.

Rivkin, Ellis. *What Crucified Jesus? The Political Execution of a Charismatic.* Nashville: Abingdon, 1984.

Robinson, John A. T. *The Human Face of God.* London: SCM, 1973.

Sanders, E. P. *Jesus and Judaism.* Philadelphia: Fortress Press, 1985.

———. *Paul and Palestinian Judaism.* Philadelphia: Fortress Press, 1977.

Schaberg, Jane. *The Illegitimacy of Jesus: A Feminist Theological Interpretation of the Infancy Narratives.* San Francisco: Harper & Row, 1987.

Schillebeeckx, Edward. *Jesus, An Experiment in Christology.* New York: Seabury, 1979.

Schweitzer, Albert. *The Quest of the Historical Jesus.* 3d edition. London: A. & C. Black, 1954.

Smith, Morton. *Jesus the Magician.* New York: Harper & Row, 1978.

Somer, Ray. *The Secret Sayings of the Living Jesus.* Waco: Word Books, 1968.

Stanton, Graham. *The Gospels and Jesus.* Oxford: Oxford University Press, 1989.

Stein, Robert H. *Jesus the Messiah: A Survey of the Life of Christ.* Downers Grove: InterVarsity Press, 1996.

Strauss, D. F. *The Life of Jesus Critically Examined.* Edited by Peter Hodgson. Lives of Jesus Series. Philadelphia: Fortress Press, 1972.

Swidler, Leonard. *Biblical Affirmations of Women.* Philadelphia: Westminster, 1979.

Taylor, Vincent. *The Gospel according to St. Mark.* New York: Macmillan, 1952.

———. *The Life and Ministry of Jesus.* London: Macmillan, 1961.

Terrien, Samuel. *Till the Heart Sings: A Biblical Theology of Manhood and Womanhood.* Philadelphia: Fortress Press, 1985.

Trocmé, Etienne. *Jesus as Seen by His Contemporaries.* Philadelphia: Westminster, 1973.

Vermes, Geza. *Jesus and the World of Judaism.* Philadelphia: Fortress Press, 1983.

——— . *Jesus the Jew: A Historian's Reading of the Gospels.* New York: Macmillan, 1973.

Wansbrough, Dom Henry. "Mark III.21—Was Jesus Out of His Mind?" *New Testament Studies* 18 (1971–72): 233–35.

Weiss, Johannes. *Jesus' Proclamation of the Kingdom of God.* Lives of Jesus Series. Philadelphia: Fortress Press, 1971.

Wenham, David. "The Meaning of Mark III.21." *New Testament Studies* 21 (1974–75): 295–300.

Wilson, Ian. *Jesus the Evidence.* London: Weidenfeld & Nicolson, 1984.

Witherington, Ben, III. *The Christology of Jesus.* Minneapolis: Fortress Press, 1990.

———. *The Jesus Quest, The Third Search for the Jew of Nazareth.* Downers Grove: InterVarsity Press, 1995.

——— . *Women in the Ministry of Jesus, A Study of Jesus' Attitude to Women and Their Roles as Reflected in His Earthly Life.* Cambridge University Press, 1984.

Wright, N. T. *Jesus and the Victory of God. Christian Origins and the Question of God.* Vol. 2. Minneapolis: Fortress Press, 1996.

Zeitlin, Irving. *Jesus and the Judaism of His Time.* Cambridge: Polity Press, 1989.

Psychological Studies

Alexander, F. and S. Selesnick, *The History of Psychiatry.* New York and Toronto: The New American Library, 1966.

Atkins, Richard. "Discovering Daddy: The Mother's Role." In *Father and Child: Developmental and Clinical Perspectives,* edited by S. Cath et al., 139–49. Boston: Little, Brown and Co., 1982.

Bainton, Roland. *Behold the Christ: A Portrayal in Words and Pictures.* New York: Harper & Row, 1974.

Bakan, David. *The Duality of Human Existence: An Essay on Psychology and Religion.* Chicago: Rand McNally, 1966.

Berkowitz, Louis. "The Devil Within." *Psychoanalytic Review* 55 (1968): 28–36.

Besdine, Matthew. "The Jocasta Complex, Mothering and Genius, Part 1." *Psychoanalytic Review* 55 (1968): 259–77.

——— . "The Jocasta Complex, Mothering and Genius, Part 2." *Psychoanalytic Review* 55 (1968): 574–600.

——. "Mrs. Oedipus." *Psychology Today* 2 (January 1969): 40–47.

——. "Mrs. Oedipus Has Daughters, Too." *Psychology Today* 4 (March 1971): 62–65.

Binet-Sanglé, C. *La Folie de Jesus.* 4 vols. Paris: Maloine, 1910–1915. Cited by Walter Bundy, *The Psychic Health of Jesus* (see below).

Boisen, Anton. *The Exploration of the Inner World: A Study of Mental Disorder and Religious Experience.* Willett, Clark & Co., 1936; reprint edition, Philadelphia: University of Pennsylvania Press, 1971.

——. "What Did Jesus Think of Himself?" *Journal of Bible and Religion* (January 1952): 7–12.

Berger, Louis. *From Instinct to Identity, The Development of Personality.* Englewood Cliffs, N.J.: Prentice-Hall, 1974.

Berguer, Georges. *Some Aspects of the Life of Jesus from the Psychological and Psycho-analytic Point of View.* New York: Harcourt, Brace and Co., 1923.

Brown, J. A. C. *Freud and the Post-Freudians.* Harmondsworth, Middlesex, England: Penguin, 1961.

Browning, Don. *Generative Man: Psychoanalytic Perspectives.* Philadelphia: Westminster, 1973.

Brye, Ilse, and Lois Afflerbach. "The Developmental Sciences: A Bibliographic Analysis of a Trend." *Mental Health Book Review Index* 16 (1971): i–xvi.

Buell, Jon, and O. Quentin Hyder. *Jesus: God, Ghost or Guru.* Grand Rapids: Zondervan, 1978.

Bundy, Walter. *The Psychic Health of Jesus.* New York: Macmillan, 1922.

Bushman, Richard. "Jonathan Edwards as Great Man: Identity, Conversion and Leadership in the Great Awakening." In *Encounter with Erikson,* edited by Donald Capps et al. (see below), 217–52.

Capps, Donald. "The Desire to Be Another Man's Son: The Child Jesus as an Endangered Self." In *The Endangered Self,* edited by Richard K. Fenn and Donald Capps, Monograph Series 2, Center for Religion, Self and Society. Princeton: Princeton Theological Seminary, 1992.

——, et al., eds. *Encounter with Erikson: Historical Interpretation and Religious Biography.* Missoula: Scholars Press, 1977.

Cath, Stanley, et al., eds. *Father and Child, Developmental and Clinical Perspectives.* Boston: Little, Brown and Co., 1982.

Chodorow, Nancy. *The Reproduction of Mothering, Psychoanalysis and the Sociology of Gender.* Berkeley, Los Angeles and London: University of California Press, 1978.

Clark, Walter Houston. *The Psychology of Religion, An Introduction to Religious Experience and Behavior.* New York: Macmillan, 1958.

Corsini, Raymond. *Current Psychotherapies.* Itasca, Ill.: F. E. Peacock, 1973.

Darroch, Jane. "An Interpretation of the Personality of Jesus." *British Journal of Medical Psychology* 21 (1947): 75–79.

Dolto, Françoise, and Gérard Sévérin. *The Jesus of Psychoanalysis: A Freudian Interpretation of the Gospel.* New York: Doubleday, 1979.

Edinger, Edward. *Ego and Archetype.* New York: Putnam, 1972.

Eisenstadt, J. Marvin. "Parental Loss and Genius." *American Psychologist* 33 (March 1978): 211–22.

Erikson, Erik. *Childhood and Society.* 2d edition. New York: W. W. Norton, 1963.

——. *Young Man Luther: A Study in Psychoanalysis and History.* New York: W. W. Norton, 1958.

——. "The Galilee Sayings and the Sense of 'I.'" *The Yale Review* 70 (Spring 1982): 321–62.

——. *Gandhi's Truth: On the Origins of Militant Nonviolence.* New York: W. W. Norton, 1969.

——. *Insight and Responsibility.* New York: W. W. Norton, 1964.

——. *Life History and the Historical Moment: Diverse Presentations.* New York: W. W. Norton, 1975.

Fisher, Seymour, and Roger Greenberg. *The Scientific Credibility of Freud's Theories and Therapy.* New York: Basic Books, 1977.

Fowler, James W. *Stages of Faith: The Psychology of Human Development and the Quest for Meaning.* San Francisco: Harper & Row, 1981.

Freud, Sigmund. *Leonardo da Vinci, A Study in Psychosexuality.* New York: Vintage Books, 1916; reprinted as *Leonardo da Vinci and a Memory of His Childhood.* New York: W. W. Norton, 1964.

——. "A Neurosis of Demoniacal Possession in the Seventeenth Century." In *Collected Papers,* vol. 4, 436–72. London: The Hogarth Press, 1956.

——. *New Introductory Lectures on Psychoanalysis.* Harmondsworth, Middlesex, England: Penguin Books, 1973.

——. *An Outline of Psycho-Analysis*. Revised edition. New York: W. W. Norton, 1949.

Fromm, Erich. *The Anatomy of Human Destructiveness*. Greenwich: Fawcett, 1973.

——. *The Dogma of Christ*. New York: Doubleday, 1966.

——. *The Heart of Man, Its Genius for Good and Evil*. New York: Harper & Row, 1964.

Furman, Erna. A *Child's Parent Dies*. New Haven and London: Yale University Press, 1974.

Garde, Noel I. *Jonathan to Gide*. New York: Vantage Press, 1964.

Gay, Peter. *Freud for Historians*. New York: Oxford University Press, 1985.

Gide, André. "Le Retourde L'Enfant Prodigue (The Return of the Prodigal Son)." In *The André Gide Reader*, edited by David Littlejohn, 379–93. New York: Alfred A. Knopf, 1971.

Gillespie, V. Bailey. *Religious Conversion and Personal Identity: How and Why People Change*. Birmingham, Ala.: Religious Education Press, 1979.

Gilmore, William J. *Psychohistorical Inquiry: A Comprehensive Research Bibliography*. New York and London: Garland Publishing, Inc., 1984.

Green, Clifford. "Bonhoeffer in the Context of Erikson's Luther Study." In *Psychohistory and Religion: The Case of Young Man Luther*, edited by Roger Johnson, 162–96. Philadelphia: Fortress Press, 1977.

Grensted, L. W. *The Person of Christ*. London: Nisbet & Co., 1933.

Haley, Jay. *The Power Tactics of Jesus Christ*. New York: Avon, 1969.

Hall, G. Stanley. *Jesus the Christ, in the Light of Psychology*. New York and London: D. Appleton, 1924.

Hatterer, Lawrence J. *Changing Homosexuality in the Male*. New York: Dell, 1971.

Horner, Tom. *Jonathan Loved David: Homosexuality in Biblical Times*. Philadelphia: Westminster, 1928.

Houghton, Rosemary. *The Liberated Heart*. New York: Seabury, 1974.

Hirsch, William. *Religion and Civilization: The Conclusions of a Psychiatrist*. New York: The Truth Seeker Co., 1912.

Jacoby, Russel. *Social Amnesia: A Critique of Contemporary Psychology from Adler to Laing*. Boston: Beacon Press, 1975.

James, William. *The Varieties of Religious Experience: A Study in*

Human Nature. New York: Longmans, Green and Co., 1902; reprint edition, London: Collier-Macmillan, 1961.

Jewett, Paul K. *Man as Male and Female: A Study in Sexual Relationships from a Theological Point of View*. Grand Rapids: Eerdmans, 1975.

John XXIII, Pope. *Journal of a Soul*. Montreal: Palm Publishers, 1965.

Johnson, Roger, ed. *Psychohistory and Religion: The Case of Young Man Luther*. Philadelphia: Fortress Press, 1977.

——— . "Psychohistory as Religious Narrative: The Demonic Role of Hans Luther in Erikson's Saga of Human Evolution." In *Psychohistory and Religion*, 127–61.

Kelly, William. "Refathering in Counseling and Psychotherapy." In *Fathering: Fact or Fable?* edited by Edward Stein, 108–38. Nashville: Abingdon, 1977.

Kern, George M. and Leon H. Rappoport, eds. *Varieties of Psychohistory*. New York: Springer Publishing Co., 1976.

Krailsheimer, A. J. *Conversion*. London: SCM, 1980.

Lamb, Michael E., ed. *The Role of the Father in Child Development*. New York: John Wiley & Sons, 1976.

Lamers, William Jr. "The Absent Father." In *Fathering, Fact or Fable?*, edited by Edward Stein, 68–86. Nashville: Abingdon, 1977.

Langer, Walter. *The Mind of Adolf Hitler*. New York: New American Library, 1972.

Lee, R. S. *Freud and Christianity*. Harmondsworth: Penguin, 1948.

Leslie, Robert C. *Jesus and Logotherapy: The Ministry of Jesus as Interpreted through the Psychotherapy of Viktor Frankl*. New York: Abingdon Press, 1965.

Levinson, Daniel. *The Seasons of a Man's Life*. New York: Alfred Knopf, 1978.

Lloyd, Raymond. "Cross and Psychosis, Part 1." *Faith and Freedom* (Fall 1970): 13–29.

——— . "Cross and Psychosis, Part 2." *Faith and Freedom* (Spring 1971): 67–87.

Lomer, George [George de Loosten]. *Jesus Christus vom Standpunkte des Psychiaters*. Bamberg: Handels-Druckerei, 1905.

Lowe, Gordon. *The Growth of Personality, From Infancy to Old Age*. Harmondsworth: Penguin, 1972.

McDargh, John. *Psychoanalytic Object Relations Theory and the Study of Religion: On Faith and the Imaging of God.* Lanham: University Press of America, 1983.

McIntyre, John. *The Shape of Christology.* London: SCM, 1966.

McKenna, David L. *The Jesus Model.* Waco, Tex.: Word Books, 1977.

Maslow, Abraham. *Religious Values, and Peak-experiences.* New York: Viking, 1964; Compass edition, 1970.

Mazlich, Bruce, ed. *Psychoanalysis and History.* Revised edition. New York: Grosset and Dunlap, 1971.

Meissner, W. W. *Psychoanalysis and Religious Experience.* New Haven: Yale University Press, 1984.

Miller, John W. *Biblical Faith and Fathering: Why We Call God "Father."* New York: Paulist Press, 1989.

———. "Jesus' 'Age Thirty Transition,' A Psychohistorical Probe." *Journal of Psychology and Christianity* 6/1 (Spring 1987): 40–51; reprinted as "Jesus and the Age Thirty Transition" in *Christian Perspectives on Human Development*, edited by Leroy Aden, David G. Benner, and J. Harold Ellens, 237–50. Grand Rapids: Baker Book House, 1992.

——— . "The Personality of Jesus as Reflected in His Parables." In *The New Way of Jesus*, edited by William Klassen, 56–72. Newton, Kan.: Faith and Life, 1980.

——— . "Psychoanalytic Approaches to Biblical Religion." *Journal of Religion and Health* 22 (Spring 1983): 19–29.

Moebius, P. J. *Rousseau's Krankheitsgeschichte.* Leipzig: F. C. W. Vogel, 1889.

Mullahy, Patrick. *Oedipus Myth and Complex, A Review of Psychoanalytic Theory.* New York: Grove Press, 1948.

Müller-Braunschwig, Carl. "Analyse eines Idealtypus des Gottesglaubens." In *Psychoanalyse und Religion*, edited by R. Nase and J. Scharfenberg. Darmstadt: Wissenschaftliche Buchgesellschaft, 1977.

Murry, J. Middleton. *Jesus, Man of Genius.* New York: Harper & Brothers, 1926.

Nachtlinger, Veronica. "Psychoanalytic Theory: Preoedipal and Oedipal Phases with Special Reference to the Father." In *The Role of the Father in Child Development*, edited by Michael E. Lamb, 277–305. New York: John Wiley and Sons, 1976.

Nase, Eckart, and Joachim Scharfenberg, eds. *Psychoanalyse und Religion.* Darmstadt: Wissenschaftliche Buchgesellschaft, 1977.

Neumann, Erich. *The Origins and History of Consciousness.* New York: Pantheon Books, 1954.

Pelikan, Jaroslav. *Jesus through the Centuries: His Place in the History of Culture.* New Haven: Yale University Press, 1985.

Peterson, Geoffrey. "Regression in Healing and Salvation." *Pastoral Psychology* 19 (September 1968): 33–39.

Pruyser, Paul. "From Freud to Erikson: Developments in Psychology of Religion." In *Psychohistory and Religion,* edited by Roger Johnson, 88–96. Philadelphia: Fortress Press, 1977.

Pye, Lucian. "Personal Identity and Political Ideology." In *Psychoanalysis and History,* edited by Bruce Mazlich, 150–73. New York: Grosset and Dunlap, 1963.

Rasmussen, Emil. *Eine vergleichende psychopathologische Studie.* Leipzig: Julius Zeitler, 1905.

Reik, Theodor. *Dogma and Compulsion, Psychoanalytic Studies of Religion and Myths.* Westport, Conn.: Greenwood Press, 1957.

Roazen, Paul. *Freud and His Followers.* New York: New American Library, 1971.

Rubenstein, Richard. *My Brother Paul.* New York: Harper & Row, 1972.

Sanford, John A. "Jesus, Paul, and Depth Psychology." *Religious Education* 68 (1963): 673–89.

——— . *The Kingdom Within.* Philadelphia: J. B. Lippincott, 1970.

Schweitzer, Albert. *The Psychiatric Study of Jesus,* with foreword by W. Overholser. Boston: Beacon Press, 1948.

Schaffer, Rudolf. *Mothering.* Cambridge, Mass.: Harvard University Press, 1977.

Socarides, Charles. "Abdicating Fathers, Homosexual Sons: Psychoanalytic Observations on the Contribution of the Father to the Development of Male Homosexuality." In *Father and Child,* edited by Stanley Cath et al, 509–21. Boston: Little, Brown and Co., 1982.

——— . *Beyond Sexual Freedom.* New York: Quadrangle, 1975.

Sorokin, Pitrim. *The Ways and Power of Love.* Chicago: Henry Regnery Co., 1967.

Sugarman, Shirley. *Sin and Madness, Studies in Narcissism.* Philadelphia: Westminster, 1976.

Tarachow, Sidney. "St. Paul and Early Christianity, A Psychoanalytic and Historical Study." In *Psychoanalysis and Catholicism,* edited by Benjamin Wolman, 143–212. New York: Gardner, 1976.

Taylor, Gordon. "Historical and Mythological Aspects of Homosexuality." In *Sexual Inversion: The Multiple Roots of Homosexuality*, edited by Judd Marmor, 140–64. New York: Basic Books, 1965.

Taylor, Vincent. "Christology and Psychology." In *The Person of Christ in New Testament Teaching*, 277–85. London: Macmillan, 1958.

Vergote, Antoine, and Alvaro Tamayo. *The Parental Figures and the Representation of God: A Psychological and Cross-Cultural Study*. Religion and Society 21. The Hague: Mouton, 1981.

Vitz, Paul C. and John Gartner. "Christianity and Psychoanalysis, Part 1: Jesus as the Anti-Oedipus." *Journal of Psychology and Theology* 12 (1984): 4–14.

Warner, Marina. *Alone of All Her Sex: The Myth and the Cult of the Virgin Mary*. London: Quartet Books, 1978.

West, D. J. *Homosexuality*. 3d edition. London: Gerald Duckworth & Co., 1968.

Wolff, Hanna. *Jesus der Mann, Die Gestalt Jesu in tiefenpsychologischer Sicht*. Stuttgart: Radius-Verlag, 1977.

Wood, Robert W. *Christ and the Homosexual*. New York: Vantage Press, 1960.

Zeligs, Dorothy. *Psychoanalysis and the Bible: A Study in Depth of Seven Leaders*. New York: Bloch, 1974.

Scripture Index

Subjects and Names Index